THE PLYMOUTH BRETHREN

THE PLYMOUTH BRETHREN

Massimo Introvigne

OXFORD
UNIVERSITY PRESS

OXFORD
UNIVERSITY PRESS

Oxford University Press is a department of the University of Oxford. It furthers
the University's objective of excellence in research, scholarship, and education
by publishing worldwide. Oxford is a registered trade mark of Oxford University
Press in the UK and certain other countries.

Published in the United States of America by Oxford University Press
198 Madison Avenue, New York, NY 10016, United States of America.

Library of Congress Cataloging-in-Publication Data
Names: Introvigne, Massimo, author.
Title: The Plymouth Brethren / Massimo Introvigne.
Description: New York : Oxford University Press, 2018. |
Includes bibliographical references and index.
Identifiers: LCCN 2017029608 | ISBN 9780190842420 (alk. paper) |
ISBN 9780190842437 (updf) | ISBN 9780190842444 (epub) |
ISBN 9780190842451 (online resource)
Subjects: LCSH: Plymouth Brethren. | Plymouth Brethren Christian Church.
Classification: LCC BX8800 .I584 2018 | DDC 289.9—dc23
LC record available at https://lccn.loc.gov/2017029608

1 3 5 7 9 8 6 4 2

Printed by Sheridan Books, Inc., United States of America

ACKNOWLEDGEMENTS

Authors know that short books have often a longer genesis than the larger ones. Summarising in a few pages complex histories and issues is never a simple work. This one is no exception. My interest in the Plymouth Brethren started in the late 1980s and took a more definite direction after conversations with the late Bryan Wilson,[1] J. Gordon Melton, Eileen Barker, and the Swiss historian Jean-François Mayer. It continued in the following decades and was greatly helped by the fact that CESNUR, the Center for Studies on New Religions, of which I am managing director, acquired a librarian himself with a Brethren background, Luca Ciotta.

My friendship with the leading historian of the Brethren in Italy, the late Domenico Maselli, dates to the late 1990s, when Maselli, who became a member of the Italian Parliament in 1994, started promoting the idea of a new law on religious liberty. This was one of Maselli's main passions for the next twenty years and a cause I was also deeply interested in. Maselli was a pastor in the oldest Italian

---

1. Dates of birth and death of all deceased individuals mentioned in the book are included in the Index of Personal Names.

Protestant denomination, the Waldensian Church, but I discovered that he had started his ministry as a member of the (Open) Brethren. This explained his encyclopaedic knowledge of all things Brethren in Italy. After years of conversations, I and Maselli joined forces to produce a popular introduction to the Brethren in Italian in 2007,[2] later translated into French. The small book was well received and forms, in many ways, the basis of this new work. Maselli wrote an introduction to Protestantism in general for the benefit of an Italian public not necessarily familiar with it, as Italy is a predominantly Catholic country and Protestants are a comparatively small minority. He also wrote very detailed chapters on the Italian Brethren. These portions, authored by Maselli, of the Italian book of 2007 have not been included here.

He died on 4 March 2016, after a long illness and could not directly cooperate with the present volume. However, this book would never have been completed without years of conversations with Maselli. The comments he made, when we were preparing the 2007 book, after reading the chapters I wrote, were crucially important and have inspired many parts of this new work also.

Happily, a new generation of scholars has now started paying attention to the Exclusive Brethren from a sociological point of view. In particular, I have benefited from conversations with Bernard Doherty, Liselotte Frisk, and Sanja Nilsson. They have also been very generous in sharing with me texts not yet published. The same applies to Bill Buntain, a specialist of Chinese Christianity, who has shared with me a fascinating unpublished manuscript on the Exclusive Brethren's dealings with China in the 1930s.

---

2. Massimo Introvigne and Domenico Maselli, *I Fratelli. Una critica protestante della modernità* (Leumann, Turin: Elledici, 2007).

ACKNOWLEDGEMENTS

This text situates the Brethren on the background of issues and controversies about fundamentalism, 'cults', and processes of mainstreaming and retrenchment in Protestant denominations. The development of my ideas on all these issues has greatly benefited from a continuous cooperation and conversation, for many years, with the already mentioned Mayer, Barker, and Melton, as well as with Rodney Stark, David Bromley, Jim Richardson, Dick Anthony, and the late Andy Shupe. The latter was also one of the world's leading experts of cases of paedophilia and child abuse perpetrated by clergy or elders of religious communities. Discussions with Shupe certainly helped situating the accusations directed against the Brethren based on a tiny number of similar incidents.

I should also, and perhaps this should have come in the first place, thank many Brethren in Italy, France, the United Kingdom, Sweden, and the United States who accepted to be interviewed and to facilitate my extensive fieldwork among congregations and schools. However, it is a tradition of the Brethren that they prefer to remain anonymous.

CONTENTS

CONTENTS

THE PLYMOUTH BRETHREN

Introduction

WHO IS AFRAID OF THE PLYMOUTH BRETHREN?

On 24 August 2016, a devastating earthquake hit Central Italy. The historical town of Amatrice was almost completely destroyed, leaving some 300 dead and 4,500 homeless. On 28 August, survivors in Amatrice found that food and beverages were available under red tents marked Rapid Relief Team (RRT), and 1,400 queued to be served. Fire and rescue vehicles came back from the most severely hit areas with their windows fully covered with dust. Volunteers emerged from the red tents to rapidly and effectively clean the windows.[1]

The RRT is a volunteer organisation created within the Plymouth Brethren Christian Church (PBCC). The PBCC is not present in the Amatrice area, and most probably the earthquake survivors did

---

1. See 'Italy—RRT Provide Meals for the Emergency Services at Operation Amatrice Aug. 2016', available at http://www.rapidreliefteam.org/italy-rrt-provide-meals-for-the-emergency-services-at-operation-amatrice-aug-2016/, last accessed 4 October 2016. In January 2017, the same volunteers appeared at the Italian site where an avalanche had destroyed a ski resort hotel in Rigopiano, Abruzzi: see 'Italy—RRT Serves Food at Avalanche Site, Rigopiano', available at http://www.rapidreliefteam.org/italy-rrt-serve-food-at-avalanche-site-rigopiano/, last accessed 31 January 2017.

not immediately understand who their Good Samaritans exactly were. In other parts of the world, where the Plymouth Brethren have a century-old presence, some might have been surprised by the RRT's activities. Plymouth Brethren are regarded by many outsiders as a very closed community, whose interaction with non-members is limited. For their neighbours, their most distinctive character is the practice of strict separation, by which they mean their refusal to share a meal with those who are not part of their fellowship.

In fact, while the RRT was established in 2013, charitable and humanitarian activities in favour of those who are not members of their community are as old as the Brethren themselves. In various historical instances, including the Irish potato famine of 1847 and the Franco-Prussian War of 1870, early Brethren mobilised themselves in favour of all the victims, members of their fellowship or not.[2]

Even earlier, Lady Theodosia Powerscourt, a significant figure for the origins of the Brethren, was active in funding the schooling of local poor children in Ireland and supported several educational and charitable initiatives in favour of the poor of all denominations.[3] Lieutenant John Blackmore established two rescue houses for 'fallen girls' from the London streets in the 1850s, with the personal support of John Nelson Darby.[4] Dr Michael Laseron, a converted Jew from Germany who later joined the so-called 'Open' Brethren, after having been active in charitable relief work during the Franco-Prussian War, led a team of

---

2. See Plymouth Brethren Christian Church, *Faith That Serves* (Chessington, UK: Plymouth Brethren Christian Church, 2013), 4–5.

3. See Alan R. Acheson, *A True and Lively Faith: Evangelical Revival in the Church of Ireland* (Dublin: Church of Ireland Evangelical Fellowship, 1992).

4. See John Blackmore, *The London by Moonlight Mission: Being an Account of Midnight Cruises on the Streets of London During the Last Thirteen Years. With a Brief Memoir of the Author* (London: Robson & Avery, 1860).

his nurses to Serbia during the Turkish-Serbian conflict of 1876. There, he attracted some criticism for his even-handed approach to the wounded of both sides, as some felt he should not have helped injured Turks too. Later, he founded a hospital and an orphanage in London.[5]

Yet, then as now, the principle of separation was a bone of contention. The Brethren were accused by some other Christians of being sectarian, short-minded, and even heretic. At the same time, many were attracted by their radical criticism of certain features of modernity, including individualism and materialism, in the name of the Gospel. Today, their alternative lifestyle continues to fascinate some and attract the criticism of others. Plymouth Brethren raise children in a traditional way and maintain their own schools, whose quality is generally recognised, while their approach to issues such as gender or sexuality is criticised in some quarters. They dress in a more conservative way than others, and do not vote in political elections.

But who are the Brethren? Where do they come from? Their origins date to the early 19th century. In the aftermath of the French Revolution and the unrest of the Napoleonic era, groups of Christians appeared in Europe from three sources: Ireland and England; Switzerland; and Italy. They dreamed of overcoming the scandal of division between Protestant churches. To this end, they gathered to break bread with all those willing to accept the Gospel of Christ and separate from evil. As so often in the history of Christianity, this utopian vision failed to unite the Protestant Church and instead gave rise to long-lasting new independent groups within Christianity.

---

5. See Brian Best and Katie Stossel, *Sister Janet: Nurse and Heroine of the Anglo-Zulu War 1879*, ed. Adrian Greaves (Barnsley, South Yorkshire: Pen & Sword Military, 2006), 42–45.

The pioneers of this movement, whose key leader was John Nelson Darby, were united by a common interest in the twin issues of the end times and the hope of a church they described as united with the Lord in Heaven and forming Christ's body on earth, but were divided on other questions. While some of Darby's companions held that the new assemblies of the so-called Brethren, and later Plymouth Brethren, should welcome Christians of any origin if they shared a common spirit and ideal, based on stringent, conservative theology; Darby was convinced that the most important issue was to separate from evil and the apostasy that held both ancient and more modern churches in its grip.

Writing in 1855 to Friedrich August Gottreu Tholuck, a well-known representative of the European evangelical revival, Darby later reminisced that 'it then became clear to me that the church of God, as He considers it, was composed only of those who were so united to Christ, whereas Christendom, as seen externally, was really the world, and could not be considered as "the church" ... The disunion of the body of Christ was everywhere apparent rather than its unity. What was I to do? ... A word in Matthew 18 furnished the solution of my trouble: "Where two or three are gathered together in my name, there am I in the midst of them." This was just what I wanted: the presence of Jesus was assured at such worship; it is there He has recorded His name.'[6]

Although the ensuing distinction between the 'Exclusive' Brethren, who followed Darby's separatism, and the 'Open' Brethren remains crucial, it does not reflect the great variations in attitude between Brethren nor the influences that the different branches had

6. John Nelson Darby, *Letters of John Nelson Darby*, second reprint of the 3rd ed. (Kingston-on-Thames: Stow Hill Bible and Tract Depot, n.d. but circa 1941), 3 vol. (Chessington, Surrey: Bible and Gospel Trust, 2005), 3:301. A first reprint of the 3rd ed. had previously been published in Holland: Winschoten, The Netherlands: Hejkoop. 1962–1963.

over one another. In 1936, the US Bureau of the Census identified six major groups, from 'Brethren I' to 'Brethren VI'.[7] Scholars of the Brethren movement were later to add four others, but the situation in Britain and the United States was not identical to that in Continental Europe. And China represented a separate and different development.

An examination of the Brethren is vital, not only as part of the history of modern Protestantism, of which they form an important component, but also in any consideration of the nature of such contested categories as fundamentalism and evangelicalism. On the other hand, scholarly literature about the Brethren is not abundant. Of Darby, historian Donald Akenson argued in 2016 that 'there is no biography that comes even close to decent scholarly standards'.[8] The same author noted that the early Brethren kept few records, if any, of their activities. They believed that the Second Advent of Jesus Christ would occur soon and were more preoccupied with evangelising than with writing down reports for the benefit of future historians. Later, some reconstructions were offered by insiders such as William Blair Neatby, whose father had been a leader of the Brethren and who had been himself a member for a while.[9] Eventually, within the Brethren movement itself, valuable, if apologetic, historical works emerged,[10] and a small network featuring both insiders and outsiders developed around the Christian Brethren Archive at the University of Manchester Library, the Brethren Archivists and

---

7. See Elmer Talmage Clark, *The Small Sects in America* (Nashville, Tennessee: Cokesbury Press, 1937), 218–223.

8. Donald Harman Akenson, *Discovering the End of Time: Irish Evangelicals in the Age of Daniel O'Connell* (Montreal: McGill-Queen's University Press, 2016), 4.

9. William Blair Neatby, *A History of the Plymouth Brethren* (London: Hodder & Stoughton, 1901).

10. See e.g., Max S. Weremchuck, *John Nelson Darby* (Neptune, New Jersey: Loizeaux Brothers, 1992).

Historians Network and its *Brethren Historical Review*, the work of independent historian Timothy C. F. Stunt, and a variety of specialised websites. Within the field of sociology, Bryan Wilson was the author in 1967 of a pioneer study and continued devoting some attention to the Brethren for several decades.[11] But the academia in general was late in paying attention, leaving the field open for controversial works criticising the Brethren first for their 'heresies' and later as part of a reactionary, anti-modern 'cult'.

What I propose here is a very short introduction to the Plymouth Brethren. As the title implies, I will focus on the Plymouth, or Exclusive, Brethren, particularly on their branch known as Brethren IV, or PBCC, mentioning the so-called Open Brethren (confusingly, also identified as Plymouth Brethren in North America) just in passing. This introductory chapter tries to highlight problems of definition: of the word 'Brethren' itself and of the important but ambiguous categories of evangelicalism and fundamentalism. Chapter 2 explores the difficult question of the origins of the Brethren, and Chapter 3 their division in different groups. Chapter 4 focuses on the group most often referred to as 'Plymouth Brethren' by the media, known as the Brethren IV in the US Census classification, which calls itself PBCC. But first, as mentioned, a short discussion of terminology is in order.

THE BRETHREN MOVEMENT

In the world of Protestantism, the term 'Brethren' is used to describe three distinct movements. The first is that established by the

---

11. Bryan R. Wilson, 'The Exclusive Brethren: A Case Study in the Evolution of a Sectarian Ideology', in *Patterns of Sectarianism: Organization and Ideology in Social and Religious Movements*, ed. Bryan R. Wilson (London: Heinemann Educational Books, 1967), 287–342.

Moravian Brethren, the disciples of the Czech reformer Jan Hus; the second began with the Lutheran-based Pietist awakening; the third, which is the subject of this work, appeared from 1820 onwards in several European countries (England, Ireland, Switzerland, and Italy).

In 1992, American sociologists Roger Finke and Rodney Stark published a seminal work, *The Churching of America*, where they proposed a model for interpreting Protestant social history taking as its starting point the element of 'protest" whether religious, political or social, which of course is at the root of the very word 'Protestantism'.[12] Throughout history, Protestant churches were born as protest movements, on the edges of the religious scene, before beginning a process of institutionalisation as soon as they acquired a stable organisational structure. The spirit of Protestantism, Stark and Finke claim, is in itself anti-institutional. Its protest is largely about the corruption it regards as inherent in large structures and institutional churches. Often in history, Protestants have proclaimed their desire to move 'outside of Babylon' and to return to the 'purity' of primitive Christianity. According to Finke and Stark's model, these 'good intentions' normally would not last long. Little by little, the second generation of each new Protestant wave will in turn start a journey toward institutionalisation.

The very name 'Brethren' is connected with this process. Not for the first, nor for the last time in Protestant history, the believers gathered around Darby regarded the existing Christian churches as hopelessly corrupted as institutions, although they still included good men and women, and emphatically denied that they were engaged in creating a new denomination. They simply called

---

12. Roger Finke and Rodney Stark, *The Churching of America, 1776–1990: Winners and Losers in Our Religious Economy* (New Brunswick, New Jersey: Rutgers University Press, 1992).

themselves 'Christians' and only gradually and with some reluctance accepted to be designated as 'Brethren' or 'Christian Brethren'. Only during Darby's last years, he came to accept the name Plymouth Brethren to distinguish his followers from other Christian groups also known as Brethren. He was, of course, aware, that the name was not entirely accurate, as the group's origins, as we will see in the next chapter, had more to do with Ireland than with Plymouth. The name Plymouth Brethren, however, stuck.

Although Darby and his friends consistently insisted that they did not want to establish a new denomination, this is how gradually Plymouth Brethren came to be perceived, at least by outsiders and scholars. But this is precisely the core of Finke and Stark's argument, and something that kept happening in the history of Protestantism. Not even Martin Luther wanted to found a Lutheran church. He believed he was simply restoring the original, primitive Christian church of Jesus Christ. Since, however, not all Christians of his time agreed with him, he ended up being at the origin of a 'Lutheran' denomination. Certainly, Plymouth Brethren's ecclesiology is far away from Lutheranism, and their resistance against institutional-isation is visible to this very day. On the other hand, the use itself of the name 'Plymouth Brethren' confirms that Darby's heirs went through a process of denominationalisation, as much as they tried to resist it.

PLYMOUTH BRETHREN AND EVANGELICALISM

The model proposed by Finke and Stark is aimed at explaining the sociohistorical evolution of Protestant *denominations*. But today many scholars would maintain that differences *between* denominations are much less important than differences *within* each denomination, chiefly between liberals and evangelicals. It is generally argued that, although in the 20th and 21st centuries Plymouth Brethren both regarded themselves and were perceived by others as separated from evangelicals,[13] Darby and his 19th-century friends had a decisive, if rarely acknowledged, influence on the whole global evangelical movement.[14]

But which Protestants, exactly, are 'evangelical?' The word, to start with, has at least three different meanings. In languages other than English, including Spanish, the word literally translating 'evangelical' both was used historically and is still used today as a synonym of 'Protestant', as opposed to 'Catholic'. Protestants, after all, claim to refer to the Gospel (*evangelium* in Latin) alone. In Spanish-speaking countries it is not unusual to come across all sorts of Protestant churches that present themselves to the public simply as '*iglesia evangélica*'.

In a second sense of the term, some 19th- and early 20th-century theologians and scholars identified as 'evangelical' denominations those who were closer to the enthusiasm of the Gospel era and reacted against the lack of warmth of older churches. This use of 'evangelical' to designate a *denomination*, perhaps less popular today, coexisted with a third use of the word, which gradually became dominant, to identify an *attitude* within a larger denomination, somewhat 'conservative' and as such opposed to 'liberal' or 'progressive'.

What is the core content of the 'evangelical' attitude? Definitions vary,[15] but both the National Association of Evangelicals in the

---

13. See Roger N. Shuff, 'Open to Closed: The Growth in Exclusivism Amongst Brethren in Britain 1848–1953', *Brethren Archivists and Historians Network Review* 1 (1997): 10–23.

14. See J. Gordon Melton, *Melton's Encyclopedia of American Religions*, 8th ed. (Farmington Hills, Michigan: Gale Research, 2009), 517.

15. See William R. Ward, *The Protestant Evangelical Awakening* (Cambridge: Cambridge University Press, 1992); David Hempton and Myrtle Hill, *Evangelical Protestantism in Ulster*

United States and the influential *Blackwell Dictionary of Evangelical Biography* in the United Kingdom adopt a definition proposed by British historian David Bebbington in 1989.[16] It has been widely adopted by scholars and is known as the 'Bebbington quadrilateral'. Interestingly, Bebbington was taken to a Brethren assembly by his parents as a child, although later he became a Baptist.[17]

The Bebbington quadrilateral introduced four criteria to identify an individual or a group as 'evangelical'.[18] First, 'biblicism': the Bible is the supreme authority of the evangelicals and is regarded as essentially infallible. Second, 'crucicentrism': by reading the Bible, evangelicals look at the atonement, or salvation offered by God to humanity through Christ's sacrifice on the Cross, as the centre of their religious experience. Third, 'conversionism': the response to the Cross should be a deep personal conversion, and those converted should in turn try to convert others. Fourth, 'activism': converting others requires a systematic and sustained effort. Evangelicals insist that this effort is missionary and aimed at saving souls, and that in fact evangelicalism is not defined by its political proclivities, although evangelical constituencies in the 20th and 21st centuries have played an increasingly important role in American and other elections.[19]

Society, 1740–1890 (London: Routledge, 1992); Mark Noll, *The Rise of Evangelicalism: The Age of Edwards, Whitefield and the Wesleys* (Downers Grove, Illinois: InterVarsity Press, 2003).

16. National Association of Evangelicals, 'What Is an Evangelical?', n.d., available at http://nae.net/what-is-an-evangelical/, last accessed 12 August 2016; Donald Lewis, ed., *The Blackwell Dictionary of Evangelical Biography*, 2 vol. (Oxford: Blackwell, 1995).

17. Eileen Bebbington, *A Patterned Life: Faith, History, and David Bebbington* (Eugene, Oregon: Wipf and Stock, 2014), 9.

18. David W. Bebbington, *Evangelicalism in Modern Britain: A History from the 1730s to the 1980s* (London: Unwin Hyman, 1989).

19. See National Association of Evangelicals, 'What Is an Evangelical?'

In fact, the missionary attitude is central for evangelicals. It is reminiscent of the comment made in 1966 by theologian Joseph Ratzinger, later Pope Benedict XVI, that in the Catholic Church the opposite of 'liberal' is not 'conservative' but 'missionary'.[20] Most evangelicals would not particularly appreciate the parallel. Although the feature is not part of the Bebbington quadrilateral, evangelicalism is traditionally anti-Catholic, or at least fiercely engaged in affirming the Protestant distinctiveness and its difference from Catholicism.

Evangelicals today are normally critical of the Plymouth Brethren, as they see the latter's separatism as an obstacle to activism and missionary work.[21] On the other hand, there is little doubt that both the Brethren emerged within the context of a pre-existing evangelical milieu and that the dominant theology of contemporary evangelicalism, particularly in the field of eschatology, has been immensely influenced by Darby and the early Brethren, although the debt is seldom acknowledged.[22] Perhaps, the Brethren are better seen as a distinctive, and somewhat idiosyncratic, 'radical expression' of evangelicalism.[23]

PLYMOUTH BRETHREN AND FUNDAMENTALISM

Plymouth Brethren found most of their early followers within the non-conformist 'Free Church' movement. These churches emerged

---

20. Joseph Ratzinger, 'Weltoffene Kirche?' in *Umkehr und Erneuerung. Kirche nach dem Konzil*, ed. Theodor Filthaut (Mainz: Matthias-Grünewald-Verlag, 1966), 291.
21. See Shuff, 'Open to Closed', 21–22.
22. See Akenson, *Discovering the End of Time*, 485–486.
23. Shuff, 'Open to Closed', 22.

in the 19th century as a reaction against State churches and, in general, against the perceived worldly and lukewarm nature of established denominations. It has often been claimed that Free Church theology is fundamentalist in nature, but everything depends on how the term 'fundamentalism' is understood. It means different things to different people. Historically, it has been used in at least three different ways.

First, the expression 'fundamentalism' was born in the 19th century to designate the position of those Protestants who defended the absolute, literal truth of the Bible. With the publication of the booklets entitled *The Fundamentals* between 1910 and 1915,[24] the expression became commonly used to describe a militant critique of liberal Protestant theology. The distinctive feature of this critique was an approach to the Bible that saw the sacred text as being supernaturally inspired in all its parts and fully authoritative. Understood in this sense, 'fundamentalism' did not refer to a distinct group of denominations, but to an attitude which could be found, to a greater or lesser extent, within all the main denominations of Protestantism. This use of the word 'fundamentalism' to designate a conservative, militant approach to theology and the Bible *within* the mainline Protestant churches fell out of favour from the 1930s onwards, when 'fundamentalism' mostly referred to the more conservative denominations, but underwent something of a revival since the 1970s, with the reappearance of 'fundamentalist' tendencies within several mainline Protestant communities, particularly in the United States.

Secondly, in the 20th century, fundamentalists' main targets were inter-Protestant ecumenism, the World Council of Churches in

---

24. 'Two Laymen', *The Fundamentals: A Testimony to the Truth*, 12 vol. (Chicago: Testimony Publishing, 1910–1915).

Geneva, and the Federal (later National) Council of Churches in the United States. Eventually, the issue became serious enough for fundamentalists within several denominations to set up new breakaway organisations. This separatist line, different from original fundamentalism that largely remained within the mainline denominations, led to the movement often being termed 'neo-fundamentalism'. Since then, fundamentalism has been used to describe a group of denominations, some of which came into being in the 1930s, while others already existed and had their origins in Europe. On the other hand, within some denominations, fundamentalists did not break away but established their own inter-church institutions and attempted, with varying degrees of success, to hold sway over the denomination as a whole. The Southern Baptists are a typical example of this process.

Thirdly, with the rise of the televangelists in the 1970s and their involvement in American political life, the term 'fundamentalism' was increasingly used over the last few decades, often polemically, to designate groups of militant conservatives, actively trying to influence the outcome of American and other elections, within a wide variety of denominations. The meaning of the term became no longer solely or essentially theological, but predominantly political. Eventually, Protestants who were active on the political right were labelled 'fundamentalists', quite independently of their theology. More generally, 'fundamentalist' came to refer to anybody who defended a religious point of view in an extreme or radical manner and was involved in conservative politics, which led to parallel uses of the term beyond Protestantism. It became common to hear expressions such as 'Islamic fundamentalism' and 'Hindu fundamentalism', although scholars cautioned against the vagueness of the label.[25]

25. See Martin E. Marty and R. Scott Appleby, eds., *The Fundamentalism Project*, 5 vol. (Chicago and London: University of Chicago Press, 1991–1995).

Conservative Protestant churches, including the Plymouth Brethren, do not necessarily have any political engagement. Some are 'fundamentalists', but only in the theological sense of holding strictly to the 'fundamentals'. The early Brethren also traditionally shared the anti-institutional and ultra-congregationalist character- istics of the world of fundamentalism, since many local churches refused to join associations, federations, or larger denominations.

The debate about the meaning of the word 'fundamentalism' has long been mostly synchronic. Attempts have been made to dis- tribute various denominations and movements on a chart, in which each is labelled as being 'fundamentalist' or 'non-fundamentalist' based on its current characteristics, without much regard to the diachronic or historical dimension. The latter dimension has been studied by the 'new paradigm' sociology of religion, which emerged in the United States since the 1990s. It used elements borrowed from economic theory to distribute religious 'demand' into mar- ket 'niches', corresponding to various types of requests and expec- tations on the part of 'religious consumers'. Based on the works of Rodney Stark, Laurence Iannaccone, and myself, five niches can be identified: ultra-liberal, liberal, conservative, fundamentalist, and ultra-fundamentalist.[26]

New paradigm sociology made two main discoveries. The first was that these niches are not all the same size: most people inter- ested in organised religion find themselves in the central, conserva- tive niche, which aims for *some* distancing from modern lifestyles, as distinct from a radical or extreme challenge to modernity. The niches on the extremes, the ultra-liberals and the ultra-fundamentalists, attract a disproportionate amount of media attention despite

26. See Massimo Introvigne, *Fondamentalismi. I diversi volti dell'intransigenza religiosa* (Casale Monferrato, Alessandria: Piemme, 2004).

having the fewest members. It is also important to draw a distinction between the fundamentalist and the ultra-fundamentalist niches. In the former, a radical *doctrinal* critique of modernity is accompanied by some *practical* compromise or accommodation. In the latter, modernity is perceived as being so intolerable that it is totally rejected, either by setting up communities that are physically separate from the rest of the world, often in isolated mountainous or desert regions, or by attempting to subvert it through armed revolution and terrorism. This distinction is relevant for the Plymouth Brethren, who may be fundamentalist but certainly are not ultra-fundamentalist.

The second discovery of the new paradigm theory is that religious movements and churches are rarely static. Over the course of their history, they move from one niche to another. Most, although not all, new religious movements within Christianity are born out of a protest against a loss of fervour in majority religions, combined with a quest to recover the lost purity of old. In other words, they are born in the fundamentalist niche. In accordance with the Finke-Stark model of mainstreaming, as they grow and come to have a majority of second- and third-generation members, these new churches normally soften their radical line and move from the (comparatively marginal) fundamentalist to the (mainstream) conservative niche. At this point, some members will feel betrayed and withdraw again to the fundamentalist niche, either creating a division or leading the whole denomination into what sociologist Armand Mauss called 'retrenchment'.[27]

It may seem that this is just a new way to describe the Weberian journey 'from sect to church'. According to Max Weber, each new

---

27. Armand Mauss, *The Angel and the Beehive: The Mormon Struggle with Assimilation* (Indiana and Chicago: University of Illinois Press, 1994).

religious form is born as a 'sect', made up of members who joined as adults and characterised by a high degree of awareness of the group's difference from the surrounding society. It eventually develops into a 'church', in which the majority of the members are born within the community, and there is less of a sense of being different.[28] But, according to the new paradigm, the opposite can also happen. A religious group can move from church to sect. Indeed, many churches—though, contrary to what might be imagined, not all of them—have a missionary emphasis and feel that it is important to increase their membership. If a church perceives that an excessive separation from the world is diminishing missionary effectiveness, it may move from the fundamentalist to the conservative niche. On the other hand, a church that has moved away from the fundamentalist niche may perceive that it did so at the price of losing doctrinal and spiritual integrity, and 'retrench' itself back to fundamentalism.

This complex dynamic is vital to an understanding of the history of the Plymouth Brethren. Born in the fundamentalist niche, some of them shifted to the conservative one. Some members could not accept this shift and remained or returned to the fundamentalist camp. As a first approximation, the traditional distinction between 'Open' and 'Exclusive' Brethren appears to correspond to the dichotomy between conservatives and fundamentalists. However, there is within the larger Brethren movement a whole range of intermediate positions. And in Plymouth Brethren history there have been periods of mainstreaming and others of retrenchment, as evidenced by the different interpretations of separatism, a key doctrinal and sociological feature of the movement.

---

28. Max Weber 'On Church, Sect, and Mysticism', English transl., *Sociological Analysis* 34, 2 (1973): 140–149.

While ultra-fundamentalist groups often resort to violence, fundamentalist groups are generally peaceable. Few in the surrounding modern society agree with their values. However, many who would never join them do appreciate their testimony against some disturbing characteristics of the modern world, including extreme individualism and widespread materialism. Moreover, with the passage of time, and if they do not find themselves in a situation of discrimination or persecution, fundamentalist groups generally end up softening their more radical characteristics and moving, albeit slowly, towards the conservative niche. Today, media tend to associate fundamentalism with political radicalism and terrorism. Movements labelled as fundamentalist are immediately perceived as dangerous. Those concerned with religious liberty should remember that the word 'fundamentalism' was born in a Christian Protestant context and originally designated a movement that was scarcely interested in politics and certainly was not violent. And it is certainly not acceptable to use fundamentalism as a label to discriminate against groups that, while critical of several aspects of modernity, maintain a law-abiding and peaceful attitude.

2

Darby and the Origins of the Plymouth Brethren

THE PROPHETIC CONTEXT

Why were the Brethren rapidly successful? Seen from their point of view, the answer is easy enough. John Nelson Darby received a special light directly from Heaven about the true nature of the church of God. Darby himself claimed as much in his 1855 letter to Friedrich August Gottreu Tholuck:

> I saw in Scripture that there were certain *gifts* which formed true ministry, in contrast to a clergy established upon another principle. Salvation, the church, and ministry, all were bound together; and all were connected with Christ, the Head of the church in Heaven, with Christ who had accomplished a perfect salvation, as well as with the presence of the Spirit on earth, uniting the members to the Head, and to each other, so as to form 'one body,' and He acting in them according to His will.[1]

1. Darby, *Letters*, 3: 300.

This truth set aside centuries of church history, and connected the Brethren directly with the first Christians, renewing the enthusiasm of Pentecost. Social historians, however, whose business is not to evaluate emic religious claims, should consider in what broader context Darby and his friends started their missionary activity and why audiences were receptive to their message.

One of the side effects of the overthrowing of the Old Regimes in the upheaval of the French Revolution, and the subsequent succession of Napoleonic wars in Europe, was to drive many Christians in both the British Isles and Continental Europe back to a fervent reading of the Scripture. The prophetic books of Daniel and Revelation in the Bible resonated with them particularly strongly during these years, which really did appear to be heralding the end of the world, with a crisis in every area of traditional values.

This distinctive climate explains the extraordinary breadth of circulation of the work of a Chilean Jesuit, Manuel de Lacunza y Díaz, *Venida del Mesías en gloria y majestad* (*The Coming of Messiah in Glory and Majesty*), the first edition of which was circulated privately in manuscript form in 1811.[2] The work was to go through no fewer than nine editions before 1826 and was translated into English by a well-known Presbyterian preacher, Edward Irving, in 1827.[3] It was immediately successful. That a book written not only by a Catholic but also by a Jesuit, became a best-seller among conservative Protestants looked so strange that some started arguing that the real author was not a Chilean Jesuit but some anonymous

---

2. Manuel de Lacunza y Díaz, *La Venida del Mesías en gloria y majestad*, ed. Mario Góngora del Campo (Santiago de Chile: Editorial Universitaria, 1969).

3. Juan Josafat Ben-Ezra [Manuel de Lacunza y Díaz], *The Coming of Messiah in Glory and Majesty*, ed. and trans. Edward Irving, 2 vol. (London: L.B. Seeley and Son, 1827).

Protestant. Yet, that it was by Lacunza has been conclusively demonstrated by modern scholarship.[4]

Irving wrote that Lacunza's prophetic argument was 'perfect and irrefragable' and that, no matter how much a good Protestant may dislike the Jesuits, 'there is no Protestant writer I know of to be at all compared to him.'[5] Irving might have taken some comfort in the fact that Lacunza was in a way a marginal Catholic. Born in Santiago de Chile in 1731, he was forced to leave the country after the Society of Jesus was banned there in 1767. Settling in Imola, Italy, in 1772, he lived a solitary life and worked on his magnum opus, which aimed to restate Christian millenarianism in modern terms. Lacunza devoted a large section to examining the Lord's Prayer, in which he contended that most Christians have no idea what they are really asking for when they pray 'Thy kingdom come' and that the second coming of Christ was imminent.[6]

Lacunza set out a distinction between the Church and the kingdom of God. For the kingdom of God to appear, the Antichrist must appear first, preceded by a general crisis in Christendom. It is hardly surprising that the events of the Napoleonic era and the French Revolution that preceded it would later be seen as initial signs that the Chilean Jesuit's prophecy was being fulfilled. Lacunza held that for the return of Christ 'in glory and majesty' to be possible, the Antichrist must first clearly manifest himself. He believed that the latter would not be a single individual, but a collective entity made up of apostate Roman Catholic clergy. This enabled him to

4. See Alfred-Félix Vaucher, 'Le Royaume de Dieu d'après le Père Lacunza', *Les Signes des temps* 1 (1935): 7–15; Alfred-Félix Vaucher, *Une célébrité oubliée. Le père Manuel Lacunza y Díaz* (Collonges-sous-Salève: Fides, 1941); Alfred-Félix Vaucher, *Lacunziana. Essais sur les prophéties bibliques* (Collonges-sous-Salève: Fides, 1955).
5. Ben-Ezra [Manuel de Lacunza y Díaz], *The Coming of Messiah in Glory and Majesty*, 1: xxvi.
6. Lacunza, *La Venida del Mesías*, 110–111.

produce an original interpretation of the relationship between the Jews and the Christian Church. He held that, after the Jews rejected the Messiah, the city of the people of God was no longer Jerusalem but Rome. The Christian Church became the assembly of God, its clergy the bride of Christ. Because the clergy fell and became apostate, however, the Jews would be restored to form the active part of the Church, and Jerusalem would once again become the focal point of the relationship between God and the world.[7] This explains why Lacunza's book was first circulated in Britain indicating as its author a 'Juan Josafat Ben-Ezra', describing himself as a converted Jew.

According to Lacunza, when the Antichrist would start persecuting the Jews who had remained faithful to God, Jesus would resurrect the believers who had died, and would meet resurrected believers and those who were still alive in the air. Hence the title of his book, 'The Coming of Messiah in Glory'. Indeed, Christ would appear to the believers in glory, overcome the apostate clergy, and reign over the earth from Jerusalem prior to the last judgement.

It would be wrong to underestimate the influence of the Chilean Jesuit's prophetic writings in the process that led many to join the Plymouth Brethren.[8] In fact, Lacunza's work was a major influence on all early British evangelicalism. It was not, however, the only source of a general and widespread interest in eschatology. For example, as early as 1813, a book by William Cuninghame, a Scottish landowner and Congregationalist minister, also stated, albeit less clearly, the theory of a second coming of Christ prior to the Millennium.[9]

7. Lacunza, La Venida del Mesías, 93–110.
8. See Harold Hamlyn Rowdon, The Origins of the Brethren, 1825–1850 (London: Pickering & Inglis, 1967).
9. William Cuninghame, Pre-millennial Advent of Christ Demonstrated from the Scripture (London: J. Hatchard, 1813).

Millenarian ideas became combined with calls to radical Christian renewal, sometimes expressed in terms of a desire for ecumenical unity between believers, and sometimes in the completely opposite terms of a strict separation between 'true' believers and 'worldly,' traditional Churches. One of the key representatives of this Europe-wide revival movement was the Scotsman Robert Haldane.[10] As well as being very active in his homeland, he was also to be one of the key figures in the Geneva, Switzerland revival known as the *Réveil*. Like his brother, James Alexander Haldane, Robert was an ordained Anglican clergyman, and it was during his ministry in the Church of Scotland that he became persuaded that for Christians to be more closely dependent on the Holy Spirit, ecumenical cooperation between Protestant churches was necessary.

In March 1821, this led to a small gathering of the representatives of several denominations, including the Anglican Daniel Wilson, who was to become Bishop of Calcutta in 1832; George Burder, a Congregationalist and secretary of the London Missionary Society; Jabez Bunting, a Methodist; and Edward Irving, who was shortly to translate Lacunza's book.

In theory, the aim of this gathering was to encourage greater cooperation between churches. However, the facts appear to speak against this being a first step towards unity. James Alexander Haldane is considered the founder of Scottish neo-Congregationalism. His brother Robert was at the origins of the Scottish Baptist movement. Irving will eventually become extremely controversial as the founder, with others, of the Catholic Apostolic Church, an idiosyncratic denomination with roots in Protestant evangelicalism, charismatic phenomena such as speaking in tongues announcing

---

10. See James Alexander Haldane, *Memoirs of the Lives of Robert Haldane of Airthrey, and of His Brother, James Alexander Haldane* (London: Hamilton, Adams and Co., 1852).

subsequent Pentecostalism, and an elaborate quasi-Catholic liturgy, which restored a college of apostles believing the end of the world will occur during their lifetime.[11]

Understandably, later Plymouth Brethren were keen to point out that they were as distant as possible from Irving's ecclesiology and style of worship. In the early 1830s, however, Irving had an important role in spreading millennial theories and prophecies among British evangelicals, and this prophetic corpus created a widespread interest in certain themes. Once he had familiarised himself with Lacunza's theories, around 1823, Irving came to accept not only the Chilean Jesuit's concept of the Millennium but also his thinking with respect to the Antichrist and the apostasy of the clergy.

Quite paradoxically, in Britain the same nostalgia for the primitive, undivided church formed the basis of the earlier experience of converts to Roman Catholicism, such as the future cardinals John Henry Newman and Nicholas Patrick Stephen Wiseman. They favoured a return to the Roman Catholic Church since they saw this path as the only means of achieving Christian unity. In the same years, at Oxford University, there was also a group of neo-Calvinists who, rather than emphasising church organisation, focused on the calling and election of individual believers. The main representatives of this movement were Francis William Newman, a famous classicist and the brother of the future cardinal, and Henry Bellenden Bulteel, rector of St. Ebbe's, Oxford.[12] F. W. Newman eventually joined the Brethren, only to leave them and become first a Unitarian

11. See Columba Graham Flegg, *'Gathered Under Apostles': A Study of the Catholic Apostolic Church* (Oxford: Clarendon Press, 1992).
12. See Rowdon, *The Origins of the Brethren*, 58–69; and Timothy C. F. Stunt, *From Awakening to Secession: Radical Evangelicals in Switzerland and Britain 1815–1835* (Edinburgh: T. and T. Clark, 2000).

and then a freethinker.[13] Among Newman and Bulteel's early follow-ers, Benjamin Wills Newton was soon to rise to prominence.[14]

Born on 12 December 1807, of Quaker parents, Newton went up to Exeter College, Oxford on 10 December 1824, where he performed brilliantly. He had previously become a member of the Church of England with a possible view to ordination. Shortly there-after, he underwent a crisis of faith as a result of which he became a Calvinist. He became deeply convinced that salvation was a gift of God, which was not given to all men, but was an individual, free work of election.[15]

In 1827, while he was working as a tutor in Ireland for the family of the famous lawyer Edward Pennefather, Francis Newman got to know his employer's brother-in-law, John Nelson Darby, who was to influence his ideas greatly.

DARBY AND THE ORIGINS OF THE BRETHREN

The British and Scottish revivals around Haldane, Irving, and the translation of Lacunza's book explain why many were prepared to accept the Brethren movement.[16] They were not, however, a direct part of its birth. Darby's approach to theological speculations

13. See Francis William Newman, *Personal Narrative in Letters, Principally from Turkey, in the Years 1830–1833* (London: The Author, 1856); Francis William Newman, *Phases of Faith; or, Passages from the History of My Creed*, 3rd ed. (London: Trübner & Co., 1874).

14. See George H. Fromow, *B.W. Newton and Dr. S.P. Tregelles, Teachers of the Faith and the Future* (London: Sovereign Grace Advent Testimony, 1959).

15. Rowdon, *The Origins of the Brethren*, 61.

16. See Timothy C. F. Stunt, 'Influences in the Early Development of John Nelson Darby', in *Prisoners of Hope? Aspects of Evangelical Millennialism in Britain and Ireland, 1800–1880* ed. Crawford Gribben and Timothy C. F. Stunt (Eugene, Oregon: Wipf and Stock, 2004), 63–66.

on the end times firmly subordinated them to the Scripture. He claimed that

> the Christian, having his place in Christ in heaven, has nothing to wait for save the coming of the Saviour, in order to be set, in fact, in the glory which is already his portion in Christ. ... Their hope of final salvation is founded on the Saviour's expiatory work, for whose return they look, according to His word. They believe the saints to be united to Him already, as the body of which He is the Head, and they await the accomplishment of His promise, expecting His coming to take them to Himself in the Father's house, so that where He is, there they may be also. Meanwhile, they have to bear His cross and to suffer with Him, separated from the world which has rejected Him. His person is the object of their faith, His life the example which they have to follow in their conduct. His word, namely, the scriptures inspired of God, that is to say the Bible, is the authority which forms their faith; it is also its foundation, and they recognise it as that which should govern their conduct.[17]

The Brethren movement's immediate origins were in Ireland, and recent scholarship emphasised its Irishness.[18] In Ireland, County Wicklow and the southern part of County Dublin were in the 1820s the set of a revival that had all the typical features of Bebbington's evangelicalism. Akenson calls this area 'Dalyland' to emphasise the leading role of Reverend Robert Daly, parish pastor of Powerscourt, in County Wicklow, for the (Anglican) Church of Ireland and later bishop of Cashel, Emly, Waterford, and Lismore. Dalyland was

17. Darby, *Letters*, 3: 298 and 305.
18. Akenson, *Discovering the End of Time*.

fiercely evangelical and committed to the dream that Anglicans, although a minority, might eventually convert the Catholic majority in their region. The evangelical luminaries, both ordained ministers and laymen (and some laywomen), most of them from distinguished families of the local aristocracy, founded several charitable and educational institutions to elevate the conditions of the rural Catholic poor—and convert them to Anglicanism at the same time.

Akenson's argument is that the Brethren emerged within the peculiar context of Dalyland and emerged because the grand dream of Daly and his friends ultimately failed. A few Catholics were converted, some of them through the ministry of John Nelson Darby, pastor of the destitute rural parish of Calary Bog. He was born in London on 18 November 1800, but his family was part of the Irish Anglican gentry and had multiple connections with the Daly circle. Darby studied at the prestigious Trinity College in Dublin, where he received a Classical Gold Medal in 1819 for his proficiency in Latin and Greek.[19] He trained as a barrister but eventually had a powerful spiritual experience that he later called his 'conversion',[20] which he dated alternatively 1820 or 1821. He abandoned the legal career and decided to become a pastor. In 1825, he was ordained first as a deacon and then as a priest in the Church of Ireland.

That he was sent as parish priest to the remote and obscure village of Calary Bog did not mean that the Church of Ireland did not hold Darby in high esteem. On the contrary, he was both well connected through family and friends to the evangelical elite of the Daly circle and regarded as a brilliant mind by his superiors. Sending him to Calary Bog was a way to put him to test in a difficult setting.[21]

19. Akenson, *Discovering the End of Time*, 128–130.
20. Darby, *Letters*, 2: 310.
21. Akenson, *Discovering the End of Time*, 210.

Anglicans in Ireland were engaged in a strong confrontation with Catholics. Calary Bog was a rough, predominantly Catholic village. Darby made an impression with his austerity. Francis Newman later claimed that 'a dozen such men would have done more to convert all Ireland to Protestantism than the whole apparatus of Church Establishment.'[22] In fact, the effective success of the ministry of Darby in Calary Bog is a matter of dispute between historians.[23] He certainly enraged local Catholics, and later received, as did others, one of the dreaded letters signed by the Catholic avenger Captain Rock, threatening that 'your life will end' should he not cease his evangelistic efforts.[24] Actually, 'Captain Rock' was not an individual but a name used in several parts of Ireland by vigilante gangs of Catholics.[25]

Darby did not regard Captain Rock as his main problem. Dalyland held him in high regard as an exemplary evangelical parish priest, but the feeling was not reciprocated. He felt that the Irish Anglicans' effort to convert Catholics was doomed by worldliness and by the Anglican hierarchy's excessive reliance on the protection of the British government. He started writing pamphlets criticising the bishops of the Church of Ireland, although at first he circulated them privately only. In 1827, Darby had what he later regarded as a providential experience, although at the time it was both physically and psychologically distressing. He had a horse-riding incident and was incapacitated for several months. Darby, however, used this time of forced inactivity for prayer and meditation, and emerged from it in 1828 ready to confront openly the Anglican hierarchy and

22. Newman, *Phases of Faith*, 27–28.
23. Akenson, *Discovering the End of Time*, 227.
24. Weremchuck, *John Nelson Darby*, 87.
25. James S. Donnelly Jr., *Captain Rock: The Irish Agrarian Rebellion of 1821–1824* (Madison: University of Wisconsin Press, 2009).

to develop a distinctive theology in the fields of ecclesiology and eschatology.

Dating these developments in a precise way is by no means easy. William Kelly, who later promoted a schism within the early Brethren, was the editor of both the first and second editions of Darby's *Collected Writings*,[26] while Darby's letters were edited by John Alfred Trench.[27] Shortly before and after World War Two, new editions of both the letters and the *Writings* were published, thanks to the effort of Hendrik L. Heijkoop, and others.[28] They in turn became the basis for the electronic editions by STEM Publishing currently used by most scholars. These collections are essential sources, yet they are not completely satisfactory for scholars. They all rely on Kelly's original work as an editor, which was guided by theological rather than philological or historical criteria. Many writings by Darby were originally published without date, and it is in attributing dates to them that Kelly has been most criticised by modern historians.[29] Plymouth Brethren themselves have tried to clarify the dating problems,[30] but many issues remain unresolved.

This is not a bibliographical question only. It makes dating with precision the separation of Darby from the Church of Ireland, the elaboration of his new theological ideas, and the beginning of the movement later known as Plymouth Brethren almost impossible.

---

26. John Nelson Darby, *Collected Writings of John Nelson Darby*, ed. William Kelly, 34 vol. (London: G. Morrish, 1866–1881); John Nelson Darby, *Collected Writings of John Nelson Darby*, 2nd ed., ed. William Kelly, 34 vol. (some of which might have been announced but never published) (London: G. Morrish, n.d.).

27. John Nelson Darby, *Letters of John Nelson Darby*, ed. John Alfred Trench, 3 vol. (London: G. Morrish, 1886–1899).

28. Darby, *Letters*, 3rd ed.; John Nelson Darby, *Collected Writings of John Nelson Darby*, 3rd ed., 34 vol. (Kingston-on-Thames: Stow Hill Bible and Tract Depot, and Winschoten, The Netherlands: Heijkoop, 1956–1971).

29. Akenson, *Discovering the End of Time*, 488–496.

30. *Dates of J.N. Darby's Collected Writings* (Chessington, Surrey: Bible and Gospel Trust, 2013).

When did Darby leave the Anglican Church? Perhaps this is not the right question. Weremchuck maintains that 'he probably never did it formally, and he could probably have resumed his ministry in the Church of Ireland at any time, had he wanted to do so.'[31] Only, he did not want to do so. During his recovery from the horse incident, between the end of 1827 and the first months of 1828, he came to the conclusion that Anglicanism as an institution was spiritually bankrupt, although he still maintained good connections with individual Anglicans for several years. In 1828, he left his position in Calary Bog. By 1834, when his father John Darby died, the young theologian regarded himself as so completely separated from the Church of Ireland that he did not attend the funeral, as he believed that Christian believers should not go to any ceremony 'where the clerical system is kept up'.[32]

What date can be regarded as the beginning of the Brethren movement is also a matter of controversy. As we shall see, breaking the bread together in commemoration of the Lord's Supper is crucially important for the Brethren. It was probably in February 1828 that Darby broke bread in Dublin for the first time with a small group of like-minded evangelical Protestants.[33] But some of its 1828 companions had already broken bread among themselves in 1827 in the same Irish city, without the presence of Darby but not without being aware of his ministry and his privately circulated criticism of the hierarchy of the Church of Ireland.[34]

31. Weremchuck, *John Nelson Darby*, 61.
32. Darby, *Letters*, 3: 479.
33. See Darby, *Letters*, 1: 383.
34. Weremchuck, *John Nelson Darby*, 64–73; Timothy C.F Stunt, 'John Nelson Darby: Contexts and Perceptions,' in *Protestant Millennialism, Evangelicalism and Irish Society, 1790-2000*, eds. Crawford Gribben and Andrew Holmes (New York: Palgrave Macmillan, 2006), 83–98.

Before introducing these early associates of Darby, we should mention another important character who is occasionally not given her due by historians of the Brethren movement, who often tend to marginalise women. Lady Powerscourt, that is, Theodosia Howard Wingfield, was the widow of Richard Wingfield, Fifth Viscount Powerscourt. She was also an ardent evangelical, and a pious socialite, who found herself at the very centre of the charitable and missionary activities promoted in County Wicklow by Reverend Daly, who was her main spiritual advisor. She was so much interested in prophecy that she travelled to Albury, England, to attend the prophetic conferences organised by Henry Drummond, from which the Catholic Apostolic Church eventually originated.[35] She liked the conferences, but disliked the theology. She replicated the conferences in her own Powerscourt estate. The first were held in 1831 and 1832 under the chairmanship of Daly, who however resigned after the second event, feeling that the conferences were attracting too many critics of the Church of Ireland. The 1833 Powerscourt conference was chaired by John Synge, a local aristocrat who remained in the Church of England but sympathised with the Brethren. The 1834, 1835, and 1836 conferences were held in Dublin.[36]

The 'Good Lady Powerscourt,' as she was called, died prematurely in 1836 at age thirty-six, probably of influenza. Although she was given a Church of Ireland funeral, during her conferences she had progressively fallen in love with Darby's theology, and possibly with Darby. Historians still debate the exact nature of any

---

35. Hamilton Madden, *Memoir of the Late Right Rev. Robert Daly, DD, Lord Bishop of Cashel* (London: James Nisbet, 1875), 150.
36. Peter L. Embley, 'The Origins and the Early Developments of the Plymouth Brethren' (PhD. diss., St. Paul's College, Cheltenham, 1966); Peter L. Embley, 'The Early Development of the Plymouth Brethren', in *Patterns of Sectarianism: Organisation and Ideology in Social and Religious Movements*, ed. Bryan R. Wilson (London: Heinemann Educational Books, 1967), 213–243.

relationship between Darby and Lady Powerscourt in the 1830s, and there is very little information about it in their writings. At least a strong oral tradition among the Brethren maintains that they intended to marry and broke the engagement for spiritual reasons, having concluded that a marriage would hinder rather than help their evangelistic activities, and that everything, including marriage, must be subjected to Darby's calling from God.[37] What is certain is that Darby was a dominant force in the Viscountess' prophetic conferences, which greatly helped him disseminate his views in Ireland and beyond.

DARBY'S COMPANIONS IN IRELAND

Who were those who broke bread together in Dublin in 1827 and associated with Darby in 1828? Most historians identify them as John Gifford Bellett, Francis Hutchinson, Edward Cronin, and the wife of one of them, probably Hutchinson's. Bellett, like Darby, had studied at Trinity College in Dublin and prepared for a career as a barrister. Unlike Darby, he practised law for a while but was independently wealthy and could spend most of his time pursuing his religious interests. He befriended Hutchinson, who was the son of Archdeacon Samuel Synge-Hutchinson, a member of the extended Synge family, which was both an important part of the evangelical circle around Daly and counted several Darby sympathisers.[38]

Bellett and Hutchinson agreed with Darby's criticism of the Church of Ireland but continued to attend its services, although they

---

37. Weremchuck, *John Nelson Darby*, 133–134.
38. Timothy C.F. Stunt, 'John Synge and the Early Brethren', *Christian Brethren Research Fellowship Journal* 28 (1976): 42–43.

also explored the dissenting denominations, at least until they first broke bread with Darby in 1828. However, Bellett and Hutchinson had started breaking bread between themselves in 1827—although, in his recollections written much later, Bellett mistakenly indicated the date of 1829—and had opened their assembly to all they regarded as sincere Christian believers, irrespective of which church they attended.[39] Soon, they learned that Cronin, a cousin of Bellett's wife, had started doing just the same as early as 1826.

Cronin was a Catholic-born dental student, and later a pioneer of homeopathic medicine, who had come to Dublin from Cork in southern Ireland. In Dublin, he had what he called a conversion experience. He decided to become a Protestant but, when it came to join a church, he felt that making such a choice would involve cutting himself off from all other denominations. He viewed 'conversion' as having made him a member of the family of Christ or, as the apostle Paul puts it, the body of Christ, which cannot be divided. He also realised that many clergy and laypersons active in various Protestant churches felt similarly uncomfortable.

Cronin thought that the way out of this predicament was to organise 'informal' meetings with others who shared his conviction that denominational barriers must be overcome. They included a deacon from a dissenting congregation that met in York Street, Dublin, Edward Wilson, who also served as assistant secretary of the Dublin Bible Society; John Parnell, the future Lord Congleton, and others, including Anglican, Congregationalist, and Baptist clergy.[40] They did not intend to set up a new organisational structure: they

---

39. Weremchuck, *John Nelson Darby*, 64–66.
40. Frederick Roy Coad, *A History of the Brethren Movement: Its Origins, Its Worldwide Development and Its Significance for the Present Day* (Exeter: Paternoster Press, 1968), 20–23.

were content to testify to their unity, which enabled them to work together even though they belonged to different churches.

This group of Christians held that the sign of unity was the Lord's Supper, instituted by Christ and shared in the form of bread and wine. The only belief that, at this stage, clearly distinguished them from institutional churches was the idea that the Lord's Supper did not have to be administered by an ordained minister. Any Christian could break the bread and serve the wine. Theirs was a deeply held conviction that the Church of God knew no divisions or barriers and that any such barriers were artificial obstacles created by human shortcomings. They also believed that these barriers should be broken down, not by merging the various leadership structures, since this would not really remove disagreement, but by mutual recognition that all believers belonged to one body.

Another early Brethren member, Anthony Norris Groves, was a dentist born in Hampshire, England, who had decided to prepare himself for pastoral ministry in the Anglican Church in order to devote himself to a mission in Asia. He went so far as to contact the Church Missionary Society, which advised him to study and take his degree at Trinity College Dublin.[41] Since he could not immediately abandon his highly successful dental practice in Exeter, he studied alongside his work, with the help of a well-educated friend, Henry Craik.[42]

It was through his visits to Dublin that Groves came into contact with Bellett and eventually abandoned his studies at Trinity

41. See Anthony Norris Groves, *Memoir of the Late Anthony Norris Groves, Containing Extracts from His Letters and Journals Compiled by His Widow* (London: James Nisbet & Co, 1857); Robert Bernard Dann, *Father of Faith Missions: The Life and Times of Anthony Norris Groves (1795–1853)* (Milton Keynes: Authentic Media, 2004); Robert Bernard Dann, 'The Primitivist Missiology of Anthony Norris Groves: A Radical Influence on Nineteenth-Century Protestant Mission' (PhD diss., University of Liverpool, 2006).
42. Rowdon, *The Origins of the Brethren*, 111–118.

College, believing that ordination was not necessary for performing God's work.[43] Groves and Bellett came to the conclusion 'that believers, meeting together as disciples of Christ, were free to break bread together, as their Lord had admonished them; and, that, in as far as the practice of the apostles could be a guide, every Lord's day should be set apart for thus remembering the Lord's death, and obeying his parting command.'[44]

Conversations between Bellett and Groves were instrumental in preparing the subsequent developments in Dublin, of which Groves, however, was not a part. He left for Baghdad via St Petersburg in June 1829, having broken bread with Hutchinson and Bellett for a few months only.[45] In Baghdad, Francis Newman and Parnell joined Groves in 1830, while Cronin accompanied Groves to a further mission to India in 1836. Groves returned to the British Isles in 1852.[46]

DARBY IN PLYMOUTH

As mentioned earlier, Francis Newman met Darby in Ireland in 1827 and was deeply impressed by him. The meeting with Darby renewed Newman's interest in the prophetic visions that he had recently derived from Irving's translation of Lacunza's book. So certain was Newman of the imminence of Christ's return that he concluded that long-term planning was futile and that, rather than pursuing a career in the Anglican ministry, he should commence an independent work of biblical research and preaching. This eventually led Newman and his already mentioned disciple, Benjamin

---

43. Weremchuck, *John Nelson Darby*, 66–69.
44. Groves, *Memoir of the Late Anthony Norris Groves*, 39.
45. Weremchuck, *John Nelson Darby*, 69; Akenson, *Discovering the End of Time*, 303.
46. On Groves' travels, see Dann, 'The Primitivist Missiology'.

Wills Newton, to accept Darby's radical critique of the established churches and leave the Church of England.

Darby, Newman, and Newton believed that the clergy had become part of the 'world' and 'in the vast majority of instances do[es] not preach the truth'.[47] For Darby and his companions, it was clear that believers should withdraw from all existing denominations, including the Anglican Church, to form independent fellowships awaiting Christ's return.

On 6 February 1831, Bulteel, who was, as we have seen, a close associate of Francis Newman and whose turn it was to preach before the University of Oxford, delivered a sermon in which he accused the Church of England of having renounced Calvinism, even though it was featured in the Thirty-Nine Articles that defined the Anglican doctrine in 1573. He then went on to denounce the Church's submission to the State.[48] Following this, a violent dispute broke out between one of the University of Oxford's most eminent professors of theology, Edward Burton, and Darby. The former held that the Church of England was Lutheran at the time of the Reformation, while Darby maintained that the main influences when the Anglican Church was formed were those of the non-Lutheran Martin Bucer and Peter Martyr Vermigli. This was not merely a historical dispute, and Darby's purpose was both to defend Bulteel and to show that his own ideas were rooted in the original spirit of the English Reformation.[49]

In the summer of 1831, Bulteel toured the west of England, preaching in the open air and in non-conformist chapels. During

---

47. John Nelson Darby, *The Notion of a Clergyman, Dispensationally the Sin against the Holy Ghost* (London: G. Morrish, 1868), 22.
48. Henry Bellenden Bulteel, *A Sermon on I Corinthians ii.12, Preached before the University of Oxford, at St. Mary's, on Sunday, Feb. 6, 1831* (London: Hatchard & Son, 1831).
49. Darby, *Collected Writings of John Nelson Darby*, 3rd ed., 3: 1–43.

his travels, he met many of those who were to play an important role in the future assemblies of the Brethren. On his return to Oxford, Bulteel found that his licence to preach in the Church of England had been revoked. This outraged his supporters and further persuaded them that separation from the Anglican Church was unavoidable.

In the late 1820s and at the beginning of the 1830s, the centre of the Brethren's activities was in Ireland. It is the Oxford debate of 1831 that explains how the Brethren came to be associated with Plymouth. It was in Plymouth that the pro-Bulteel party counted its strongest supporters, including Francis Hall, at that time a coastguard commander, and George Vicesimus Wigram, also from the University of Oxford, and whose second name, meaning 'twentieth' in Latin, indicated that he was indeed the twentieth child of his father. While still busy with Lady Powerscourt's prophetic conferences in Ireland, Darby, together with Newton, decided to settle in Plymouth. Wigram, Hall, Darby, and Newton began an itinerant preaching tour in the region. With money belonging to Wigram, at the end of the year they purchased an abandoned chapel and started to hold meetings there on Monday evenings. Sunday worship including the breaking of bread was soon being observed, privately at first and then publicly, giving birth to the first genuine assembly of the Brethren.

This new fellowship, composed of 'converts' from various origins, was organised very freely, allowing different believers to take part in preaching, prayer, and, more generally, all the activities of the Church, which was led not by an ordained minister but by Newton and Darby, who were simply known as 'elders'. It entered into a relationship with other assemblies which had sprung up here and there, bringing together people from several backgrounds, some of them Quakers dissatisfied with the increasingly rationalist turn of their Society. Newton's background was Quaker.[50]

These groups identified themselves as Brethren, but the epicentre of the movement led to them being known as Plymouth Brethren or 'Plymouthists.' From the very beginning, Newton and Darby made the Plymouth assembly 'separatist' in nature, based on the principle that believers were to 'separate themselves from evil'.[51]

Contacts were also made with groups of Brethren that had appeared in London, including one in Orchard Street, under the leadership of Wigram, who had settled there, and in Devon, as well as with free churches that had established themselves in the meantime in Switzerland, particularly in Geneva and the Canton of Vaud. One of the members of the Orchard Street Church was the Italian expatriate Teodorico Pietrocola Rossetti, who will become a central figure in the birth of the Brethren in Italy.[52] In 1837, Darby travelled to Switzerland to strengthen these new contacts. He also preached in France, in the Ardèche, while Plymouth remained under the leadership of Newton and a new assembly was established in Bristol.

MÜLLER AND THE BRISTOL GROUP

The new group in Bristol was led by two associates of Groves, Henry Craik and a young German pastor, Georg (later Anglicised as George) Müller, who was born in Prussia in 1805 and had studied

---

50. Timothy C. F. Stunt, *Early Brethren and the Society of Friends* (Eugene, Oregon: Wipf and Stock, 2015).

51. Embley, 'The Early Development of the Plymouth Brethren', 213–243.

52. Timothy C. F. Stunt, 'The Via Media of Guicciardini's Closest Collaborator, Teodorico Pietrocola Rossetti', in *Piero Guicciardini (1808–1886): un riformatore religioso nell'Europa dell'Ottocento. Atti del Convegno di studi, Firenze, 11–12 aprile 1886*, ed. Lorenza Giorgi and Massimo Rubboli (Florence: Olschki, 1988), 155.

at the University of Halle, where he was influenced by the Lutheran revival movement known as Pietism.

From Pietism, Müller brought to Bristol both a peculiar idea of conversion, understood as a radical, instantaneous change of life-style, and a literalistic approach to the Bible. He also inherited from German Pietism such a deep sense of an individual relationship with God that he ruled out any kind of dependency on other men, including financial dependency, and concluded that pastors should accept no salary.[53] In 1825, while still a student at Halle, Müller began to consider a career as a missionary and felt it was his duty to fulfil this calling among the Jews.

The idea that Israel would be restored as a nation in Palestine was a constant of Pietism, particularly Prussian Pietism. Müller's mentor at Halle had been Tholuck. Müller arrived in London in 1828, right at the time when echoes of Darby's first experiences in Dublin were being heard and talked about there.

During the early days of his time in England, Müller was so enthusiastic in his work on Hebrew and Chaldean that he spent up to twelve hours a day in study. This had a detrimental effect on both his physical and emotional health, which had also been affected by his military service in the Prussian army. It was during a convalescent trip to Teignmouth in 1829 that he had the experience that completely transformed his life. He attended several meetings in a Baptist church and was overwhelmed by what he was to refer to as his 'second conversion'.

As a result of this experience, he accepted the supreme authority of Scripture, the Calvinist doctrines of election, limited atonement

---

53. See George Müller, *A Narrative of Some of the Lord's Dealings with George Müller, Written by Himself*, 6 vol. (London: published by the Author, 1881); Arthur Tappan Pierson, *George Müller of Bristol* (London: James Nisbet & Co., 1899) [2nd ed., 1907]; Nancy Garton, *George Müller and His Orphans* (London: Hodder & Stoughton, 1963).

(the theory that the efficacity of Christ's death for salvation is limited to the elect), and the perseverance of the saints, as well as the idea of the return of Christ prior to the Millennium and the need for a more intense personal relationship with God. He also became friends with Craik, one of Groves' closest companions who, having refused to follow the former dentist to the mission field, had settled in Teignmouth, where he worked as a tutor in a private home. In a chance encounter in 1830, Müller met Groves' sister, from whom he received reports from the Asian mission, which he read with avid interest, and who was soon to become his wife. During this period, Müller took part in several informal meetings among friends to break bread together, including the one in Exeter where he met his future bride. The friendship between Müller and Craik was very important to both men. They had much in common, first and foremost a taste for study. Craik was undoubtedly more educated than his colleague. He was a talented speaker and had a remarkable knowledge of Hebrew and Chaldean, as can be seen from his work entitled *Principia Hebraica*.[54]

When he took up his studies again in London, Müller quickly realised that it would be very difficult to start a ministry amongst the Jews. This would involve submitting to a more qualified minister, as was the custom in the London Society for Propagation of Christianity among the Jews, with which he planned to work for this mission. He did not want to do this, as he believed that a preacher of the Gospel should depend on God alone. He left the missionary organisation and took up a pastoral charge in Kensington on the conditions that he was to be free to relinquish it whenever he

---

54. Henry Craik, *Principia Hebraica; or, Easy Introduction to the Hebrew Language, Exhibiting, in Twenty-four Tables, the Interpretation of All the Hebrews and Chaldee Words, Both Primitives and Derivatives, Contained in the Old Testament Scriptures*, 2nd ed., revised (London: Samuel Bagster & Sons, and Bristol: W. Mack, 1863).

deemed appropriate, and that he was not to receive a regular salary, something he felt could adversely affect his independence
and to which, as mentioned earlier, he was contrary as a matter of
principle.[55]

In 1832, Müller settled in Bristol with Craik to oversee two
independent chapels. It was there that the two friends felt the need
to hold informal meetings, over and above their pastoral work, in
which participants would take it in turn to read the Bible, pray, and
celebrate the Lord's Supper in what they deemed to be the apostolic fashion, that is, by breaking bread and drinking wine without
there being a predetermined person officiating. In 1834, on Müller's
initiative, the Bristol group founded The Scriptural Knowledge
Institution for Home and Abroad, which was to meet its needs by
'faith and labour of love' alone and 'assist Day-Schools, Sunday-
Schools, and Adult-Schools, in which instruction is given upon
Scriptural principles'. Day-schools' teachers were required to be
upright individuals, while Sunday schools and adult schools were to
be led by 'believers'. Second, the Institution's goals included spreading the Holy Scriptures, by selling modestly priced Bibles and New
Testaments to the poorer classes and, in the event of extreme poverty, freely supplying a 'cheap edition'. In general, however, Müller
was opposed to the idea of distributing free copies of the Bible, for
fear that its worth would not be properly appreciated. Third, the
Institution assisted missionaries 'whose proceedings appear to be
most according to the Scriptures'.[56]

Müller and Craik's work in Bristol featured several characteristics that were similar to those of the Brethren movement. They
came into direct contact with the Plymouth and Dublin groups

55. Rowdon, *The Origins of the Brethren, 1825–1850*, 116.
56. Müller, *A Narrative*, 1: 111–113.

when Darby visited Bristol in 1835. Meanwhile, in 1836, Müller's work in Bristol took on another dimension, with the opening of an orphanage, which was based on the model set out in the work of German Pietist, August Hermann Francke. This initiative on the part of Müller, which appeared to his friends as nothing less than miraculous, has given rise to an extensive hagiography in English. At first, no committee was set up to support Müller in his efforts, but he received so many gifts that by 1846 he could purchase land on which to build a house, which became the property of a Müller Foundation. In June 1846, Müller received a single gift totalling £1,000, another totalling £2,000 in July, and two others of £1,000 in January 1847. These gifts spurred him to still deeper commitment: he set up a committee whose aim was to finance the orphanage and help missionaries throughout the world. On 26 May 1850, the new house at Ashley Down was home to 225 children and a total of 308 people in all. This was to be only one step towards a still larger development: on 12 November 1857, a second house opened with a capacity of 400 children. In 1870, the orphanage comprised a total of five houses, two thousand children, and all the staff needed for care, teaching, and administration.[57] The Bristol orphanage is evidence that, since the very beginning, Brethren were concerned with social welfare rather than with evangelisation only.

We have spent some time looking at the expansion of Müller's work because of its international and interdenominational influence. It also played a crucial role in the growth of the Plymouth Brethren movement. Among Müller's friends and followers, there were many well-educated, wealthy people. Despite its radical nature, the embryonic Brethren fellowship was not an unsophisticated movement of marginal believers. In fact, almost all the founders of the movement

---

57. See Garton, *George Müller and His Orphans*.

were members or former members of the clergy, whether Anglican (Darby), Lutheran (Müller), or Calvinist (Rochat, to whom we will turn shortly), and had the benefit of good theological training. In other words, this was an elite movement, in which typical romantic concepts combined with a desire for Christian unity.

For Müller and his friends, the plague of ecclesiastical divisions, the growing influence of rationalism, and the shortcomings of contemporary Christianity in general had their origin in the creation of chains of dependency between individuals. By contrast, believers, redeemed by the Lord, were to form a brotherhood that relied solely on God. This was the basis of the refusal of both Müller and the missionaries in Mesopotamia and India in Groves' circle to accept a salary. Their ideal was never to create the economic links of dependency common to ministers of religion, which, according to Müller and his companions, were at the root of the corruption of the clergy. This was, again, the idea of unpaid ministry, connected to the notion, characteristic of the European *Réveil* in general, of a strict separation of Church and State. Of course, the fact that many in this circle were well-off made pursuing the ideal easier.

THE DEVELOPMENT OF DARBY'S MINISTRY

After his experiences in England, Darby received an invitation to visit French-speaking Switzerland in 1837. He was very warmly received there, at least initially, and began to review his own thoughts on ecclesiology and eschatology, refining views which he had already expressed in part in Ireland and England. Some apologetic biographies of Darby give the impression that he formulated once and for all his theology shortly after he separated for the Church of Ireland. In fact, his theological ideas evolved gradually. He explained himself that 'even though the whole truth is given to us, we apprehend it in part only. Because we apprehend truth in detail, we never have the whole at once; the character of our knowledge is such that it lays hold of different truths singly. As we lay hold of one truth, it flows into the understanding of the next, and so on.'[58]

By the time he arrived in Geneva, Darby was convinced of the doctrine interpreting history as a series of divine interventions, each with different provisions and laws, that he termed 'dispensations'. Each of these dispensations failed because of human apostasy. This was the case for Adam and Eve in the Garden of Eden, for Israel, and also for the Church. God would ultimately triumph, not in the present age of the Church, but in a future dispensation. A number of conclusions derived from this view.

In the Garden of Eden, humans sinned, but God's promise to Adam and Eve with respect to the Serpent (the devil) remained: 'And I will put enmity between thee and the woman, and between thy seed and her seed; it shall bruise thy head, and thou shalt bruise his heel' (Genesis 3:15). It was the basis of the continuing presence of a 'faithful remnant' on Earth. After the flood, this remnant consisted of Noah and his family, who were destined to repopulate the earth. Following the incident of the Tower of Babel, humanity was condemned to be dispersed, but Abraham represented the new remnant, destined to become the dispensation of Israel. This too failed, but a fresh remnant appeared again on earth, made up of those who, through the Gospel of Jesus Christ, had rediscovered the kingdom of God.

During his time with the Apostles, Jesus gave them the laws of his kingdom. Darby, however, saw these laws as not being applicable to the present Church. They belonged to another, heavenly

---

58. Weremchuck, *John Nelson Darby*, 60.

dispensation rather than to the earthly dispensation in which the Church lives. The Church was a parenthesis that appeared because of the death and resurrection of Christ. Darby also distinguished different characteristics within the person of Jesus: the Messiah; the Son of God, who was to reign on earth; and the Son of Man, who died for humankind. He assigned to the economy of the kingdom the two former characteristics, and to the economy of the Church the latter.[59]

Darby's commentary on the Lord's Prayer is clear: 'Thy will be done on earth as it is in heaven' is perfect obedience. Universal subjection to God in heaven and on earth will be, to a certain point, accomplished by the intervention of Christ in the millennium, and absolutely so when God shall be all in all.' Meanwhile, 'the prayer expresses daily dependence, the need of pardon, the need of being kept from the power of the enemy, the desire of not being sifted by him, as a dispensation of God, like Job or Peter, and of being preserved from evil.' This prayer also 'is adapted to the position of the remnant; it passes over the dispensation of the Spirit, and even that which is proper to the millennium as an earthly kingdom, in order to express the right desires, and speak of the condition and the dangers of the remnant until the Father's kingdom should come.'[60]

The echoing of early millennial themes resonates here, just as the earthly nature ascribed to the Millennium is impossible to miss. However, Darby's position led to actual divisions because of his doctrine of the ruin of the Church. Darby started out with the Pietist notion of the Church as a fellowship of individuals, which

59. John Nelson Darby, *Reflections on the Ruined Condition of the Church, and on the Efforts Making by Churchmen and Dissenters to Restore It to Its Primitive Order* (London: G. Morrish, 1841).
60. John Nelson Darby, *Synopsis of the Books of the Bible*, new revised ed., 5 vol. (London: G. Morrish, 1867), 3: 60.

exists in all Christian denominations and which forms Christ's heavenly body. However, his study of the Acts of the Apostles and the epistles of Paul, in which he saw the development of the true doctrine of Christ, finally led him to adopt the conviction that the Church was made up only of individual assemblies free from any association with the pre-existing denominations.[61]

The Lord Jesus Christ, Darby believed, entrusted the Apostles with the care and government of the Church. At the end of the apostolic era, however, troublesome spirits entered the Church and ruined it, beginning with the corruption of its hierarchy. Previous theories of the unfaithfulness of the clergy were broadened to include the whole Church, and this from the end of the first century. Darby shared Irving's view of an apostolic Church but, unlike Irving, denied the possibility of its restoration in modern times.

The earlier position of Cronin, Groves, Müller and others was thus effectively overturned. No longer could the Church be said to be living in a diaspora among the different Protestant confessions, its unity still capable of being restored. It should rather be concluded that the Church no longer existed. The dispensation of the Church had failed, just as the dispensation of Israel had failed before. Only a remnant remained, and its first duty was to separate itself from a Church that was no longer worthy of its name.

Darby believed that the remnant should not establish another denomination, which would be doomed to failure from the outset, but create local assemblies of the elects, which were to await the end of the present dispensation and the glorious return of Christ. The promise of Jesus according to which 'where two or three are gathered together in my name, there am I in the midst of them' (*Matthew* 18:20) provided necessary and sufficient grounds for

---

61. Shuff, 'Open to Closed'.

their existence. The foremost duty of these assemblies of Brethren for Darby was that of separating themselves from the 'world', this being understood to include both the existing churches and anyone who fell into errors of doctrine or practice.[62]

Darby believed that within each Christian there were two natures that had nothing in common between them: the 'old man' and the 'new man'. He was so convinced that belonging to the 'remnant of the Church' was the direct work of God who elects his own, that he decided that the main purpose of the Church was the remembrance of the death of Christ through the Lord's Supper. This weekly celebration lies at the foundation of the Brethren's social interactions and relationships. Quoting 2 Timothy 2, which states 'Let him that names the name of the Lord, withdraw from iniquity', the Brethren jealously and strictly regarded that sacred event as central to their lives and excluded from it those they regarded as either not following the true doctrines of the Gospel or not acting in accordance with them.

The consequence of this doctrine was that Brethren rejected all fellowship with any other Christian community. The practical consequences of this separatism were extremely serious and led to divisions within the Plymouth movement.

CONTINENTAL BRETHREN: SWITZERLAND AND ITALY

Why, exactly, did Darby go to Switzerland in 1837? While the radical movements we have been describing were developing in England, similar small groups were appearing in French-speaking

62. Coad, *A History of the Brethren Movement*, 124–126.

Switzerland during the confrontation between the mainline and state-supported Reformed Church of Geneva, by that time thoroughly rationalistic, and followers of the evangelical *Réveil*.[63]

For the present purposes, it is enough to mention the importance of the visit to Geneva in 1817 of Robert Haldane. Indeed, it was at Haldane's initiative that a first group of 'awakened' believers was formed, made up of dissidents from the Reformed Church of Geneva. After the Scot had left, his place in Geneva was taken by Henry Drummond, whom we mentioned in connection with the Catholic Apostolic Church. The Geneva dissidents rapidly consolidated, organising themselves into a fellowship on 23 August 1817 and having their base at Bourg-du-Four.[64] They replaced traditional presbyterianism with a collegial church leadership, entrusted to pastors and elders.

With Drummond's financial support, the Bourg-du-Four fellowship expanded its evangelistic efforts in France and beyond. It opened a small school for evangelists known as the Institut du Bourg-du-Four. Later, having grown stronger despite being the theatre of lively arguments, the fellowship also acquired new premises in the chapel of La Pélisserie, inaugurated on 24 March 1839.

In the meantime, around 1820, related groups made up of dissidents from the national church had also emerged in the Canton of Vaud. Known as the 'Ancienne Dissidence' (Old Dissent), they were guided by the Rochat brothers, Auguste and Charles, pastors in Rolle and Vevey respectively. The cantonal government had begun persecuting these groups: as a reaction, the well-known

---

63. Léon Maury, *Le Réveil religieux dans l'Église Réformée à Genève et en France (1810–1850). Étude historique et dogmatique* (Paris: Fischbacher, 1892).
64. Émile Brocher, *Notice sur l'Église évangélique libre de Genève publiée à l'occasion du cinquantenaire de sa fondation* (Geneva: Église évangélique libre de Genève, 1871).

Memorandum in Favour of the Freedom of Worship by the young Lausanne theologian Alexandre Vinet was published.[65]

After the revolutionary uprising of 1830, the *Réveil* group grew both in Geneva and in the rest of Switzerland, leading to the creation in 1831 of the Société Evangélique de Genève in opposition to the rationalism-ridden state church. This Society also opened a theological college in 1832, which was later to play a significant role in the birth of the Brethren in Italy and France, as both Italian and French elders trained there.

From 1843 onwards, the Société Evangélique de Genève had a large preaching venue at its disposal, known as the Oratoire. There was, however, a difference between the Oratoire and the chapel of La Pélisserie. The Oratoire had the sole aim of promoting a revival, seeking to touch members of the national church and more generally the population of Geneva. In contrast, the chapel of La Pélisserie wanted to rebuild the original Church of Jesus Christ on biblical, apostolic foundations. It was an assembly that preached the independence of the Church with respect to the State and the formation of 'true believers' on the old Anabaptist model. It also expressed feelings quite similar to the English and Irish Brethren.

During his first stay in Switzerland (1837–1845), Darby was in contact both with the chapel of La Pélisserie and the Old Dissent in the Canton of Vaud, at that time led by pastors Auguste Rochat and François Olivier. At first, Darby was welcomed enthusiastically by both communities. However, disagreements were later to appear because, rather than working towards the growth of these existing fellowships, Darby preferred to form new assemblies that were more closely linked to his principles.

---

65. Alexandre Vinet, *Mémoire en faveur de la liberté des cultes* (Lausanne: The Author, 1826).

A full-blown dispute broke out in 1840, following the publication of a pamphlet by Darby, in which the English preacher claimed that not only the historic churches but also the new dissident ones should recognise their apostasy and ruin. The argument was that, since the Church as a whole had become apostate in apostolic times, it was impossible for it to be revived by any means.[66] This work by Darby led to a rebuttal by Auguste Rochat, to which Darby immediately responded, also attacking the 1841 *Report of the Société Evangélique de Genève*.[67] The dispute became more bitter after a series of publications by both sides, including one by Olivier. Although the split was not yet formally declared, it was already irreparable.

Darby left Switzerland for a period during 1842, but in 1844 he launched a French-language periodical, *Témoignage de la Parole*. Meanwhile, following a 'fraternal conference' in September 1842, those who disagreed with Darby decided to promote a separate organisation. Eventually, the Église Evangélique Libre de Genève was registered in September 1848. It was in contact with 'Continental Brethren' in Italy, France, Germany, and Austria, although in all these countries there were also those who sided with Darby.

One of the correspondents of the Swiss dissidents was Italian Count Piero Guicciardini, later to become one of the foremost figures of Italian and European Protestantism, whose position was similar to that of the Brethren and the Bourg-du-Four fellowship.[68] His approach to Scripture was no different from the confident literalism that we have seen as being typical of the British Brethren.[69] Important for the origins of the Brethren movement

---

66. Darby, *Collected Writings*, 3rd ed., 1: 213–245.

67. Rowdon, *The Origins of the Brethren, 1825–1850*, 207–214.

68. See Stefano Jacini, *Un riformatore toscano nell'epoca del Risorgimento: il conte Piero Guicciardini, 1808–1886* (Florence: Sansoni, 1940); Giorgi and Rubboli, *Piero Guicciardini*.

69. See Daisy Dina Ronco, *Per me vivere è Cristo. La vita e l'opera del Conte Piero Guicciardini nel centenario della sua morte* (Fondi, Latina: UCEB, Unione Cristiana Edizioni Bibliche, 1986).

in Italy was also the presence of a Protestant Italian fellowship in London, led by Salvatore Ferretti, a distant relative of Pope Pius IX (Giovanni Maria Mastai Ferretti), and a former Catholic priest who had fled to Geneva with a woman he hoped to marry. In Switzerland, he met Darby and became convinced that there was a need for an independent ministry in Italy along the lines of the British Brethren. He left Switzerland for England, where he first busied himself establishing an institute for destitute Italian children wandering the streets of London. Later, in 1847, he founded the periodical *L'Eco di Savonarola,* which was published until 1860.

Ferretti started a Protestant fellowship among Italian expatriates in London, whose members were to include not only other refugees from the Roman Catholic clergy but also some fairly well-known political exiles from the democratic camp, including the artist Filippo Pistrucci and the literate Gabriele Rossetti from Vasto (Abruzzi), who had fled the kingdom of Naples after the Carbonari insurrections of 1820–1821 and was the father of the famous Pre-Raphaelite painter Dante Gabriel Rossetti.[70]

Italian political developments led to Guicciardini also choosing exile in London, and this was decisive for the subsequent development of the Brethren movement in Italy and other European countries, given the Florence aristocrat's prominence in international evangelical circles. The Italian Protestant fellowship in London played a much more important role in the history of the Brethren in general from the time when Guicciardini arrived there. It was in London in 1853 that he won over the Italian political radical

70. See Valdo Vinay, *Evangelici italiani esuli a Londra durante il Risorgimento* (Turin: Claudiana, 1961).

Teodorico Pietrocola Rossetti, a cousin of Gabriele Rossetti,[71] to his ideas. T. P. Rossetti returned to Italy in 1857, preaching in Piedmont with the permission of the local government and founding several churches, including the one in Spinetta Marengo, which was to become one of the centres of the Brethren in Italy. Darby visited Italy several times, as part of an international activity that led him to extended missionary trips to Europe, the United States, Canada, New Zealand, and Australia.[72]

A network of free churches gradually spread all over Italy, although it eventually divided between the followers of Guicciardini and Rossetti and those of Alessandro Gavazzi, a former Catholic priest, who favoured a centralised structure of the newly formed Italian church and also maintained a more direct involvement in politics.[73] In 1870, there were some sixty Brethren-style churches in Italy, twenty-three of which followed Gavazzi into the Free Christian Church (singular), while the others, known with a name only slightly different, Free Christian Churches (plural), remained with Guicciardini and Rossetti. In 1904, in the midst of a spiritual and financial crisis, Gavazzi's church was dissolved. Most of its local churches were absorbed by the Methodists. Meanwhile, the Free Christian Churches had taken the name Free Christian (Brethren) Churches in 1880, later to become Christian Brethren Churches.

When Rossetti and Guicciardini died, respectively in 1883 and 1886, they left behind them a growing movement, which, expanding from northern and Central Italy, also spread

---

71. See Daisy Dina Ronco, *Crocifisso con Cristo. Biografia di Teodorico Pietrocola Rossetti dalle lettere* (Fondi, Latina: UCEB, Unione Cristiana Edizioni Bibliche, 1991).
72. See Domenico Maselli, *Tra risveglio e millennio. Storia delle Chiese cristiane dei fratelli 1836–1886* (Turin: Claudiana, 1974).
73. See Giorgio Spini, *L'Evangelo e il berretto frigio. Storia della Chiesa cristiana libera in Italia, 1870–1904* (Turin: Claudiana, 1971).

remarkably in the South, particularly through the conversion of a number of railway workers in Foggia, an important southern railway junction. These railwaymen travelled throughout the southern and central region, doing the work of evangelists even as they did their jobs.[74] The Christian Brethren Churches effectively became the Italian branch of the international Brethren movement, which in the 20th century experienced the same division between Exclusive and Open Brethren that manifested itself in other countries. Most Italian churches sided with the Open Brethren, although the Exclusive branch also maintained a presence in the country.[75]

THE SPLIT BETWEEN OPEN AND EXCLUSIVE BRETHREN

Even before Darby left for Switzerland, differences had emerged between him and Newton within the Plymouth assembly,[76] which was starting to lose some of its original style. By 1834, when he briefly returned to England, Groves seems to have noticed as much: '[Groves, according to his second wife Harriet Baynes] had great sympathy and communion with the people of God in Bristol, and in the North of Devon, and thankfully ministered among them; and he visited, for a short time, the brethren at Plymouth. Here he

---

74. See Luigi Berzano and Massimo Introvigne, *Il gigante invisibile. Nuove credenze e minoranze religiose nella provincia di Foggia* (Foggia: NED, 1997), 151–158.
75. See Domenico Maselli, *Libertà della parola. Storia delle Chiese Cristiane dei Fratelli 1886–1946* (Turin: Claudiana, 1978).
76. See Jonathan D. Burnham, 'The Controversial Relationship between Benjamin Wills Newton and John Nelson Darby' (PhD. diss., University of Oxford, 1999); Jonathan D. Burnham, *A Story of Conflict: The Controversial Relationship Between Benjamin Wills Newton and John Nelson Darby* (Eugene, Oregon: Wipf and Stock, 2004).

found less comfort, feeling that their original bond of union in the truth as it is in Jesus, had been *changed* for a united testimony against all who differed from them.'[77]

The Plymouth Brethren were now emphasising separation from the apostate churches and not, as had been the intention of the first members, the dream of uniting all members of the family of Christ. In fact, the two positions were difficult to reconcile, even if many did not seem to realise this at first. Groves had perhaps been the first to become aware of the difficult coexistence of these two opposing components. Indeed, he based his ecclesiology on the traditional concept of the Church as being made up of local, autonomous congregations but innovated in his application of this view by making it an instrument of unity rather than separation. He was just as forthright as his Brethren in Plymouth in his refusal to recognise the various Christian denominations as legitimate institutions, but he was ready to work with various local congregations, even when they were part of denominational structures. If Groves deemed the spirituality of a group to be genuine, he felt that external forms were of secondary importance. Broadly speaking, he adopted the concept formulated by Ignatius of Antioch: 'where Christ is, there the Church also is.'[78]

In their work in Bristol, Müller, and Craik shared Groves' position, though they were too busy with running their churches, missionary organisations, and orphanages to concern themselves with doctrinal disputes. Controversies were, however, soon to erupt within the Plymouth community, leading to open conflict between the two streams that had originally made up the Brethren movement.

---

77. Groves, *Memoir of the Late Anthony Norris Groves*, 356.
78. Coad, *A History of the Brethren Movement*, 120.

Darby's thinking was shaped by a predominant interest in eschatology and the conviction that the Church, as a spiritual reality, was by now in ruins. This theory lies at the origin of all his other doctrines. Conversely, the Bristol Brethren, and Groves, acted on the belief that the Church, although scattered, was fully present wherever a sincere local congregation met, even if the latter was part of an institutional church, so long as the Gospel was preached there and Christ was loved. Groves explained: 'I therefore know no distinction, but am ready to break the bread and drink the cup of holy joy with all who love the Lord and will not lightly speak evil of His name.'[79]

Groves and Müller reiterated their reasons for not joining established churches: 'As bodies, I know none of the sects and parties that wound and disfigure the body of Christ; as individuals, I desire to love all that love Him. Oh! When will the day come, when the love of Christ will have more power to unite than our foolish regulations have to divide the family of God.'[80] 'I am so sure of the truth of those blessed principles the Lord has taught me, that I glory in their propagation. Simple obedience to Christ alone; recognition of Christ alone in my brother, as the Alpha and Omega of terms of communion; lastly unreserved devotion to Christ alone.'[81]

Groves also maintained that, within the Brethren movement, there should be no central authority and some doctrinal variations between different local assemblies should be tolerated. In 1833, he pointed out that some years earlier, a 'Mr. D' (who may have been Darby or, more likely, James George Deck, at that time a strong advocate of infant baptism) had invited him to refrain from preaching

79. Groves, *Memoir of the Late Anthony Norris Groves*, 48.
80. Groves, *Memoir of the Late Anthony Norris Groves*, 48–49.
81. Groves, *Memoir of the Late Anthony Norris Groves*, 321.

on baptism, on which their views were different, and had requested another brother not to publish his tract against war so as not to be assimilated with the Quakers. Groves concluded: 'Surely, if we are not free to follow all, where they follow Christ and His will, we have only changed one kind of bondage for another. I do not think we ought to propose to be modelled *unlike* every sect, but simply to be like Christ; let us neither seek nor fear a name. I wish rather to have from every sect what every sect may have from Christ.'[82]

A pacifist emphasis was present among some Plymouth Brethren from the outset. Groves made no attempt to defend himself against the accusation of having adopted the refusal to bear arms from the Quakers, indeed he virtually boasted of the fact. Similarly, he imported his ideas on adult baptism from the Baptists. However, he maintained that neither pacifism nor different ideas about baptism should become a source of division between brothers.

The assembly in Plymouth, meanwhile, was set on a completely different path. At the head of a fellowship of over 700 souls, both Darby and Newton condemned all existing ecclesiastical structures, stating they were incompatible with the New Testament Church and believers should separate from them completely. Groves replied on several occasions, and, finally, in a highly significant letter sent to Darby on 10 March 1836, he set out their points of difference once and for all.[83] He showed how far he now was from the position held by Darby who, although he would agree with Groves that there were genuine believers within the mainline churches, refused any possibility of reforming denominational structures.

Darby and Newton emphasised the importance of studying the Book of Revelation, something they themselves had undertaken

---

82. Groves, *Memoir of the Late Anthony Norris Groves*, 31.
83. Coad, *A History of the Brethren Movement*, 287–291.

in a cultural climate influenced by the studies by Lacunza and Irving. The latter's interpretation held that, apart from the opening chapters, the Book of Revelation announced events which were to take place soon and which would be related to the manifestation of the kingdom of God on earth. Darby attempted to harmonise this view with several passages of the Scripture that hinted at a two-stage return of Christ: the first, secret return would be to rapture the Church and take it to Heaven; the second would be to publicly restore the Jews to their past glory and begin a thousand-year reign. This enabled Darby to preserve his concept of multiple dispensations, with the idea of a heavenly kingdom for the Church and an earthly kingdom for the Jews. Gathered in Palestine, the Jews would go through a terrible time of great tribulation, connected with the manifestation of the Antichrist, at the end of which the promises of the Old Covenant would be fulfilled in the Millennium.

For Newton, the division between the heavenly and earthly kingdoms automatically entailed a clear separation between the economy of the Old Testament and that of the New Testament, and even two completely different paths to salvation. In the periodical *The Christian Witness*, the mouthpiece of the Plymouth group, a violent dispute broke out right from the first issue in January 1834, which then continued in several pamphlets until 1838. That year, Newton put forward the theory according to which dispensations were not necessarily completely independent, as Darby held, but could also coexist alongside each other in time. This was his attempt to reconcile the new interpretation of Revelation and Scripture with the traditional theories of the Reformation. However, the fact that Darby was far from Plymouth at the time meant that the dispute remained nothing more than an academic discussion and did not deteriorate into open hostility.

Throughout this time, Newton was leading the community in Plymouth in his capacity as elder. He allowed other members to take part in the ministry, although he exercised strict control over those who could preach, because he could not see how it was possible to allow complete anarchy in a fellowship that had become so large. On his return to Plymouth in 1845, Darby announced that he intended to leave the assembly because of the prevailing 'disorder'. He therefore did so, accompanied by a group of followers, without a formal separation. Three years later, Newton—who, it must be said was not always as clear as he might have been—appeared to be questioning Christ's divinity in an oral commentary on the Psalms, summaries of which were being circulated. After repeated attempts to persuade Newton to withdraw these commentaries failed, the Brethren loyal to Darby decided that separation from Newton was unavoidable.

When Müller's fellowship in Bristol, meeting at Bethesda Chapel, refused to agree with this separation and, by welcoming two people from Newton's fellowship to the Lord's Table, effectively chose to remain neutral as to Newton's teaching on the person and sufferings of Christ, Darby and his supporters separated from Müller too. In later years, this was always referred to by Darby's followers as the Bethesda Question and made a test of fellowship for them.

Following this rupture, the movement thus split into three parts, which were to go increasingly separate ways, under the respective leadership of Newton, Darby, and Müller. They had real and deep differences in ecclesiology. Like Groves, Müller did not subscribe to the remnant theory nor to the theory of the ruin of the Church, seeing the fruit of the work of Christ as being the establishment of a Church that, though invisible in the present day, was being formed in preparation for the return of Christ, and which became material and visible around the signs of the Lord's Table. There, sincere believers were welcome irrespective of whether or not they continued to worship in the mainline churches. Darby practiced both primary and secondary separation, that is, he not only refused to break bread with those who remained in the 'apostate' churches or subscribed, like Newton, to theories he regarded as heretical, but also remained strictly separated also from those that, although not personally guilty of any heresy, did not practice the principle of separation with respect to persons and communities considered by Darby as heretic.

Newton, meanwhile, moved right away from the Plymouth Brethren. In 1864, he wrote in a very revealing letter to the Italian preacher Luigi De Sanctis, a copy of which was in the personal collection of historian Domenico Maselli, that he had been separated for the last sixteen years and more from the 'Brethren' or 'Plymouthists' and that he was resolutely opposed to their doctrines. The sixteen years mentioned by Newton in 1864 date the separation to 1848. This is the date of the split between the Open Brethren, ready to welcome good Christians of any origin or denomination to their services, and Exclusive Brethren, who practiced Darby's strict doctrine of separation. Other divisions were to follow.

Darby died in Bournemouth on 29 April 1882, a few months after having completed his *Introduction to the Old Testament*. Although divisions are relevant in the Brethren's history, they should not obscure the immense evangelical activity of Darby, particularly through the international and transatlantic tours he undertook in the last part of his life. Nor should Darby's influence beyond the Brethren be underestimated. His translations of the Bible, particularly of the New Testament, which have been explored in a 2015 doctoral dissertation by Gilles Despins,[84] remains to this day an

---

84. See Gilles Despins, 'A Critical Assessment of J.N. Darby's Translation Work' (PhD diss., South African Theological Seminary, 2015).

important reference for conservative English-speaking Protestants throughout the world. The two main conservative Bible colleges in the United States, Moody Bible College in Chicago and the Dallas Theological Seminary, were deeply influenced by Darby's ideas. American historian J. Gordon Melton wrote that 'probably no Christian thinker in the last two hundred years has so affected the way in which English-speaking Christians view the faith, and yet has received so little recognition of his contribution, as John Nelson Darby.'[85]

85. Melton, *Melton's Encyclopedia of American Religions*, 8th ed., 517.

Trinity College, Dublin, John Nelson Darby's alma mater.
Photo by Massimo Introvigne.

John Nelson Darby.
Courtesy of the Archives of the Plymouth Brethren Christian Church.

The Powerscourt Estate, County Wicklow, Ireland, where Lady Powerscourt's theological conferences were held.

Photo by Massimo Introvigne.

Home in Fitzwilliam Square, Dublin, where Darby first broke bread with the early Brethren.

Photo by Massimo Introvigne.

Frederick Edward Raven.
Courtesy of the Archives of the Plymouth Brethren Christian Church.

James Taylor Sr.
Courtesy of the Archives of the Plymouth Brethren Christian Church.

James Taylor Jr.
Courtesy of the Archives of the Plymouth Brethren Christian Church.

Kellyville Hall, NSW, Australia, a typical Brethren IV's meeting hall.
Courtesy of the Archives of the Plymouth Brethren Christian Church.

Street preaching by Brethren IV in London, 2016.
Courtesy of the Archives of the Plymouth Brethren Christian Church.

Self-directed learning in a Brethren IV school, 2016.
Photo by Massimo Introvigne. (For privacy reasons, school authorities have asked me not to indicate in which school the picture was taken.)

The Brethren's Rapid Relief Team in action at the Italian site of the Rigopiano avalanche disaster, January 2017.

Courtesy of the Rapid Relief Team (RRT).

3

Raven and the Time of Divisions

A Map of the Brethren Movement

THE DIVISIONS OF THE BRETHREN GROUPS

Melton pointed out that, in order to draw up an inventory of the Brethren and their multiple divisions, three methodological principles must be considered. Firstly, it must be recognised that no inventory will be exhaustive to the point of reflecting the full breadth of the legacy passed down by the three main streams of 19th-century Brethren, which derived, as we have seen, from Darby, Newton, and the Müller-Groves group. The typical Brethren ideal of each congregation being autonomous, and their suspicion of denominational structures, meant that each merger and fusion was followed by new separations. In addition to the main groups, there are hundreds of autonomous congregations that have no intention of organising themselves above the local level. Secondly, concerning Darby's heritage, Melton maintains that a distinction must be drawn between his theology and his ecclesiology. In the United States, for instance, Darby's theology has been adopted by dozens of churches, preachers, and universities, right across a broad spectrum that covers everything from fundamentalism to conservatism. However, many of those who adopted portions of Darby's theology, particularly his eschatology, 'never accepted the ecclesiology nor became Brethren, a fact that often gave Darby and his followers moments of consternation.'[1] Darby's consternation was all the more pronounced because his six journeys to Canada and United States between 1862 and 1877 did not succeed in resolving the issue.[2] There are still millions of conservative and fundamentalist Christians in the United States who have been influenced by Darby, but the membership of explicitly 'Darbyite' congregations numbers only a few thousands there.

Lastly, Melton also underlines the need, when describing the Brethren, to refrain from two opposite temptations. The first is to minimise the differences between 'Darbyism' in its stricter sense, a label that should best be reserved to Exclusive Brethren only, and the approach of Müller and Groves, which led to the Open Brethren. In fact, these differences are genuinely profound in nature. The second temptation is to reduce the complexity of the contemporary Brethren movement to the distinction between its Open and Exclusive wings only. In fact, elements of Darbyite theology have penetrated groups generally held to be Open. Furthermore, groups of fellowships regularly shift from one category to another. In addition, there are groups of Brethren that are very difficult to categorise.[3]

In the 1920s and 1930s, the US Bureau of the Census, which was collating religious statistics since the beginning of the 20th

1. Melton, *Melton's Encyclopedia of American Religions*, 8th ed., 520.
2. From his letters and writings, we know that Darby's six visits to Canada were from September 1862 to September 1863, from October 1864 to August 1865, from July 1866 to Spring 1868, in July 1870, from August or September 1872 to March 1873, and from July 1876 to June 1877, on his return from Australasia. During all these visits, except the short one in July 1870, he also travelled to United States. He was in the United States from August 1862 to October 1863, from Spring 1865 to June or July 1865, from July 1866 to February or March 1868, from June 1872 to April 1873, from September 1874 to August 1875 (on his way to Australasia) and from June 1876 to March 1877 (on his return from Australasia).
3. Melton, *Melton's Encyclopedia of American Religions*, 8th ed., 521–522.

century, was confronted with the problem of classifying the different Brethren subgroups. The problem was made even more difficult by the fact that many Brethren fellowships throughout the United States refused to give themselves a name, on the basis that such a practice would not be biblical. The Bureau concluded that the problem could be solved by putting together a classification using Roman numerals. This classification first emerged in 1936, with a list which extended from Brethren I to Brethren VI.[4] It was adopted by some historians of American religions, including Elmer Talmage Clark and Arthur Carl Piepkorn. The latter added four new categories, from Brethren VII to Brethren X.[5]

Problems arise when the Bureau of the Census categories are transposed to Europe, where some of the American groups are not present. The numeral categories are often reproduced in simplified form by users who are sometimes unaware of their origin. For instance, the expression 'Brethren I', which in the US Bureau of the Census classification designated the group started by Frederick W. Grant, is often used with varying degrees of precision by European authors to designate Darbyite fellowships that do not belong to any of the other groups. The situation remains somewhat confused. But it is not impossible to attempt to untangle at least its knottier aspects.

BRETHREN I AND THEIR SCHISMS
(BRETHREN VII AND BRETHREN VIII)

As mentioned earlier, the Brethren I label is often used in Europe to denote all locally or nationally independent Brethren

---

4. Clark, *The Small Sects in America*, 223.
5. Arthur Carl Piepkorn, 'Plymouth Brethren (Christian Brethren)', *Concordia Theological Monthly* 41 (1970): 165–171.

communities that do not wish to be part of any national or international network. They include the communities that separated themselves from Darby after his controversy with Newton. Eventually, Newton left the Brethren movement altogether and organised independent congregations whose members, after his death in 1899, mostly joined the Baptists.[6] In 1866, however, William Henry Dorman accused Darby of having been contaminated by Newton's Christological heresies and separated from him. Dorman's independent assemblies are included by some scholars among Brethren I but never gathered a significant number of followers.[7]

In the United States, the Bureau of the Census classification identified Brethren I with a different group, which separated from Darby in 1879. The origins of these Brethren I lie in a controversy which emerged in 1879 in Ryde, on the Isle of Wight. There, due to questions about the morality of certain members, some had left and set up an independent meeting. Edward Cronin, a member of the Kennington assembly in London whom we already met, visited Ryde and broke bread with these 'independents'. This raised the immediate question of which gathering in Ryde should be recognised as in fellowship with the larger Brethren community. While the Kennington assembly was slow to act, the London Park Street meeting recognised Cronin's action as divisive, and he and those who had followed him were declared out of fellowship. Eventually, Kennington also took the same action. The controversy extended to Ramsgate where some endorsed Cronin's actions, and in turn that assembly became divided. After two years, the

---

6. Coad, *A History of the Brethren Movement*, 151.
7. Alfred Wellershaus, *Die Wahrheit Gottes und die Widerstände dagegen: Ein Überblick über die Geschichte der Brüder* (Gütersloh: Brüderbewegung, 2010), 9. [1st ed., 1937].

Park Street assembly recognised the group that refused Cronin's actions, but this decision was not accepted by William Kelly, an influential leader from Blackheath, London. Several other prominent Brethren supported Kelly, resulting in a division throughout United Kingdom in 1881.[8]

The Kelly party survived for several decades in England. It eventually merged with Brethren III. In the United States, one of the foremost disciples of Darby at the time of this controversy was Frederick W. Grant. After having initially accepted the 1881 decision disfellowshipping Kelly, Grant questioned the principle according to which one body could decide matters for a number of assemblies within a city and put dissenting members out of fellowship. Grant argued that by acting thus, the Church of the Lord was structuring itself according to notions and boundaries that were similar to those of boroughs and municipalities, derived from secular authority and certainly not coming from God. Secondly, major metropolises were large enough to be considered as countries in their own right; coordinating Brethren activities in a city the size of London or New York was not really that different from setting up a national denomination in Belgium or the Bahamas. This, Grant argued, ran directly contrary to the Darbyite idea that local assemblies should not be subject to national ecclesiastical authorities.

There were also theological issues. Grant held that converted sinners were immediately saved and received the Holy Spirit at the moment of conversion, an idea prevalent in American revival movements, while Park Street and Darby held that salvation could only be obtained after a person had reached a proper understanding of the Gospel. Grant also maintained that the Old Testament

8. Wellershaus, *Die Wahrheit Gottes*, 10.

saints had received the eternal life in the Lord when they died, while Darby maintained that they had obtained it only with the coming of Jesus.[9]

We can regard Grant's position as a typical expression of American individualism, and he had clashed openly with Darby during meetings in 1881. Grant was also influenced by the theology of the revivals in the United States, which insisted on the sudden, individual experience of being 'born again', a theology quite foreign to Darby's ideas. The London elders of the 1880s concurred with this analysis. They sent Lord Adalbert Percival Cecil and Alfred Mace to North America in 1884, two years after Darby's death. They confirmed that Grant was actively propagating his ideas and helped the Brethren conclude that his theology was unsound. Eventually, the Brethren in Montreal judged him outside the fellowship. However, a significant proportion of the Brethren assemblies in the United States, Canada, and the West Indies followed Grant and separated from the British Brethren. It is this faction that the 1936 Bureau of the Census classification decided to identify as Brethren I.

Individualism unavoidably moved Brethren I towards the Open Brethren (Brethren II). After Grant's death, most of the assemblies that had sided with him started discussing such a move. In the meantime, they had to endure the Brethren VII split, which occurred in 1928 after a dispute between two Philadelphia businessmen, both of whom were members of the local Brethren I assembly. Each accused the other of improper behaviour and demanded that his rival be put out of fellowship. This affair was complicated by the visit of a respected English representative of the Brethren VI, or Glanton faction (to which we shall return), James Boyd, who sided

9. See Frederick W. Grant, *A Divine Movement and Our Path with God To-day* (Los Angeles: Good Tidings Publishers, 1897).

with one of the two businessmen. Boyd also defended a theological stance that had previously led to several people being excommunicated from the Brethren I: the theory that Jesus Christ did not have a 'human spirit' but only a 'divine spirit'. The leadership of Brethren I, which represented a movement born out of an aversion to centralism and excommunication, did not go so far as to put Boyd's followers out of fellowship. Those who disagreed with this ruling and who accused Boyd of heresy, however, left to set up Brethren VII, which existed independently until 1953, at which time they merged with Brethren III.[10]

Apart from the Boyd incident, Brethren VII were protesting the drift of Brethren I towards the Open Brethren. Paradoxically, their separation encouraged this drift, since those Brethren I who joined Brethren VII, about one-third of the total, constituted the faction that was the most virulently opposed to the Open Brethren. Once they had left Brethren I, the merger could proceed more quickly. By 1935, most Brethren I assemblies had joined Brethren II on the basis of decisions by each independent fellowship. However, especially in the rural areas of the United States, another movement opposing dialogue by Brethren I with the Open Brethren, that is, Brethren II, emerged in the 1920s. This 'traditionalist' remnant of Brethren I rejected any reunion with Brethren II. It was later classified by Piepkorn as Brethren VIII.[11] Like Brethren VII, Brethren VIII eventually merged with Brethren III, to the extent that it can be said that Brethren I are now extinct as a category, but are nonetheless at the origins of some of the liveliest North American fellowships, most of whom now form part of the Open Brethren (II), with a minority belonging to the faction known as Brethren III.

10. Piepkorn, 'Plymouth Brethren (Christian Brethren)', 170.
11. Piepkporn, 'Plymouth Brethren (Christian Brethren)', 170.

BRETHREN II

At the risk of oversimplification, it can be said in summary that those who feature as Brethren II in American censuses make up the main, although not the sole, stream of the Open Brethren. They descend from the group which, at the time of the 1848 separation, sided with Müller and Groves against Darby and Newton.[12] In Italy, the majority of Brethren recognise Guicciardini and Rossetti as the founders of the movement in that country and also belong to Brethren II. The same is true for Switzerland and the Church of La Pélisserie and its successors.

Brethren II, or Open Brethren, are not the main focus of this book, which is about the Exclusive Brethren, particularly Brethren IV and their schisms. The name 'Plymouth Brethren' is now generally reserved to Exclusive Brethren, although many American Brethren II congregations both accept and use it, adding to the terminology confusion. For the purpose of this study, it would be enough to mention some general features of Brethren II, which are also relevant for the evolution of the Brethren movement in general. The main problem of Brethren II is one of organisation. Local fellowships are highly suspicious of any national structure, all the more so of international ones. However, some structures above the local level have proved indispensable to coordinate financial and missionary activities and relationships with political authorities.

The difficult coexistence between an anti-institutional tradition and the need for some institutionalisation determined two schisms within Brethren II. They originated from the British

---

12. See Harold Hamlyn Rowdon, *Who Are the Brethren and Does It Matter?* (Exeter: Paternoster Press, 1986); Harold Hamlyn Rowdon, 'The Problem of Brethren Identity in Historical Perspective', in Giorgi and Rubboli, *Piero Guicciardini (1808–1886)*, 159–174.

congregations more opposed to national and international structures. In 1889, the first of these schisms led some one hundred assemblies connected with the periodical *The Needed Truth*, and known by the same name (Needed Truth Brethren), to separate from the others. They use also the names Churches of God in the Fellowship of the Son of God, the Lord Jesus Christ; and Churches of God in the British Isles and Overseas; and still maintain a separate existence in the United Kingdom, the United States, Canada, Trinidad, Jamaica, and Australia, with a significant missionary development in Malawi, Nigeria, India, and the Philippines (see their website www.churchesofgod.info). Needed Truth Brethren are the only Brethren group with a semi-presbyterian system, with elders, who 'appoint deacons and from the deacons choose new elders', having 'powers similar to that of presbyters in the Presbyterian Church'.[13]

The second schism happened in 1904, when for the first time the establishment of an international, or at least inter-British, agency aimed at coordinating domestic and missionary activities was suggested.[14] Both this schism and several American congregations of the Needed Truth Brethren were eventually reabsorbed into the main body of Brethren II.[15]

These divisions over the course of the history of Brethren II are perhaps less significant than their worldwide expansion, carried out by cohorts of missionaries, who transformed an entity comprising a few thousand believers into the present constellation of assemblies,[16] spread over 130 countries, with over 25,000 local

---

13. Melton, *Melton's Encyclopedia of American Religions*, 8th ed., 527.
14. Napoleon Noel, *The History of the Brethren*, 2 vol. (Denver: W. F. Knapp, 1936); Embley, 'The Origins and the Early Developments of the Plymouth Brethren'.
15. J. Gordon Melton, *Encyclopedia of American Religions*, 6th ed. (Detroit: Gale, 1999), 506.
16. Tim Grass, *Gathering to His Name. The Story of Open Brethren in Britain and Ireland* (Milton Keynes: Paternoster, 2006).

fellowships.[17] Estimates of membership vary between one and two-and-a-half million, depending on how 'members' are counted and what congregations exactly are regarded as part of the Brethren II network. An internal source in 2015 distinguished between 'baptised believers' (1,667,144) and regular 'adult attenders' to the meetings (2,116,838).[18] There are also several semi-independent fellowships originating from the missionary work of Brethren II. A significant example is the Evangelische Christengemeenten in Vlaanderen, which was born in Belgium and the Netherlands in the 1970s out of the efforts of Canadian Brethren II missionaries with a Flemish family background, and evolved into a quasi-denomination with some twenty-five local churches.[19]

Among Brethren II, leadership of local congregations is entrusted to elders. Some work for the church full time, while others also have a secular job. Infant baptism is not practiced, except within some American assemblies that have entered Brethren II from Brethren I. Brethren II insist that they represent a middle way between liberalism and fundamentalism, but there is an ongoing debate in their circles about the identity of the movement within Protestantism. Brethren II are aware that the primitive dream of Groves, of gathering all true believers in the Gospel together in a single structure transcending all denominations, is not on the agenda, at least not in human terms. However, unlike other branches of the Brethren, they remain willing to cooperate with other Christians, at least within certain limits, with the same spirit of openness which led to their

17. Partnership UK, 'News Release', available at http://www.partnershipuk.org/qwicsitePro2/php/docsview.php?docid=1659, 2013, last accessed on 9 August 2016.
18. Ken Newton and Jeanette Newton, *The Brethren Movement Worldwide: Key Information 2015* (Lockerbie, UK: OPAL, 2015), xxiv.
19. See Thomas J. Marinello, *New Brethren in Flanders: The Origins and Development of the Evangelische Christengemeenten Vlaanderen, 1971–2008* (Eugene, Oregon: Pickwick Publications, 2013).

separation from Darby. Thus, in the United States there are Brethren who are open to work with parachurch organisations bringing together Christians from several denominations for a common purpose, including Billy Graham's evangelistic crusades, the Gideons, and the Full Gospel Business Men's Fellowship International. The latter group includes many Roman Catholics, a fact that led Brethren II in countries other than the United States to regard their participation in the Fellowship as inappropriate. In the United States, Brethren II wishing to serve a fellowship full time are steered in the direction of conservative Protestant theological colleges, such as the Dallas Theological Seminary or the Fuller Theological Seminary in Pasadena, California. Most Brethren II vote in political elections, although members of some particularly conservative congregations refuse to do so, and some of them became members of the national Parliaments in Italy and New Zealand.

BRETHREN III AND THEIR SCHISMS (BRETHREN V, VI, AND IX)

Brethren III may in some respects be seen as a relatively old group, inasmuch as they claim to be the direct heirs to Darby's legacy, a claim that puts them in competition with Brethren IV. Among the early Brethren, the elders of the larger London assemblies gradually started to act as arbitrators for doctrinal issues that had also arisen in other towns. A turning point in this respect took place three years after Darby's death in 1882. A group led by Clarence Esme Stuart was excluded from fellowship by the London Brethren in 1885. Some documents refer to him by the name 'Charles', but he was indeed baptised 'Clarence', before his mother apparently began calling him 'Charles' within the family circle, due to his resemblance to the King of England Charles I.[20] Stuart's group survived for several years in the United Kingdom and gained a significant following in Australia and New Zealand. In the United States, it established fellowship contacts with Grant's Brethren I, although no merger took place. After Stuart's death in 1903, almost all the members of the English party merged with Brethren VI (the Glanton faction), whilst the Australians, New Zealanders, and Americans joined Brethren VII (i.e., the conservative dissidents from Brethren I) in 1931.

Unlike several adventurers of the same name, Stuart was indeed distantly related to the English royal family. He held that for redemption to be complete, Christ was required not only to shed his blood on the Cross but also to formally and ritually offer it to the Father in Heaven between the time of his death and that of his resurrection. In the eyes of the Reading assembly, this obscure doctrine was not grounds for putting Stuart out of fellowship, but a minority group, consisting mainly of women, who could not accept this, left the Reading assembly. Brethren in other assemblies then had to judge whom in Reading they accepted as being in fellowship. This issue, and others, reinforced the principle established in the 1848 Bethesda issue, that fellowship was one and a judgement in one assembly affected all the others. In practice, many smaller meetings deferred to the London Brethren, who in this case regarded Stuart as out of fellowship, and he had to set up a separate movement.[21]

In this process, which hinted at the role of a final instance for deciding doctrinal controversies among the Brethren, the key figure was Frederick Edward Raven, the leader of the Greenwich Fellowship in London who stands at the origins of Brethren IV. He was born 9 September 1837 at Saffron Walden, Essex. Raven

---

20. 'Clarence Esme Stuart: Biography', n.d., available at http://www.newble.co.uk/writers/Stuart/biography.html, last accessed 9 August 2016.
21. W.R. Dronsfield, *The 'Brethren' since 1870* (Lowestoft, Suffolk: The Author, 1965), 33–34.

was raised in the Church of England, but he left it and joined the Brethren in 1865 after a personal meeting with Darby. Raven had a very distinguished career in the British Admiralty. In 1873, he was appointed Secretary of the Royal Naval College. He held this position for twenty-five years and served as Secretary of the Council of Naval Education. Raven rose to prominence among the Brethren as an authoritative preacher.[22] He also met with opposition, centred in 1888–1890 on theological issues about the notion of eternal life.[23] It was a typical conflict between those who saw themselves as guardians of the orthodoxy as set out in Darby's teachings and others who felt they must be ready for fresh light vouchsafed by the Holy Spirit. This opposition resulted in the Brexhill meeting excluding Raven, leading to a division that he had not sought. Most of the London assemblies, including the one in Park Street, took the side of Raven and originated the group later known as Brethren IV.

Raven's adversaries, Brethren III in the US Bureau of the Census' terms, are known in Great Britain as the 'Lowe Brethren' after the name of Raven's chief critic, William Joseph Lowe. Lowe's excellent relationship with the Exclusive Brethren assemblies,[24] founded by English missionaries in Continental Europe, explains why Brethren III are sometimes also known as 'Continental Brethren'. Indeed, most Exclusive Brethren south of the English Channel sided with Lowe, particularly after a conference in Elberfeld, Germany, in 1890, where attending German, Swiss, and Dutch Brethren decided to uphold the Bexhill decision excluding Raven.[25] However, in no European countries was the attitude unanimous, and some

---

22. See Frederick Edward Raven, *Ministry by Frederick E. Raven: New Series*, 21 vol. (Kingston-on-Thames: Stow Hill Bible and Tract Depot, 1965–1968).

23. Wellershaus, *Die Wahrheit Gottes*, 12–14.

24. *A Brief Account of the Life and Labours of the Late W. J. Lowe* (London: C.A. Hammond, 1928).

25. Wellershaus, *Die Wahrheit Gottes*, 16.

congregations remained with Raven. Others went even further in their condemnation of Raven and separated from the Brethren III, accusing them of maintaining elements of the Raven system. They included Rudolf Brockhaus, the son of the most influential German leader of the Brethren, Carl Brockhaus.[26] Some 600 members of his 'Alte Elberfelder' Brethren still exist in Germany, and their conferences attract several thousand sympathisers.

In 1890, Brethren III were defined first and foremost as being 'anti-Ravenite', in other words in terms of their opposition to a doctrine (or a person) rather than their positive proclamation of one. Their own doctrine could be distinguished by a quest for a full Darbyite orthodoxy and a stringent, ultra-precise exegesis of the English preacher's writings. Paying a quasi-philological degree of attention to every detail of Darby's writings inevitably led to further controversies over apparently minor episodes, reinforcing Raven's opinion that, even as they were proclaiming faithfulness to Darby, Brethren III were building the rigid ecclesiastical hierarchy he had always refused. On the other hand, Brethren III continually sought unity with all those who refused both what they saw as the excessive liberalism of the Open Brethren, or Brethren II, and the notion of referring to the authority of a living teacher typical of Raven and Brethren IV.[27]

A typical example of this attitude among Brethren III can be seen in the 1905 incident of Alnwick, Northumberland.[28] In 1904, nineteen Brethren in Alnwick decided to hold independent meetings, only joining the rest of the local community for the breaking of bread. In January 1905, those who appeared to be the leaders of

26. Wellershaus, *Die Wahrheit Gottes*, 17–19.
27. See R[aymond] K[enneth] Campbell, *Reunited Brethren: Brief Historical Account Including a Brief Statement of Some Vital Principles of Faith* (Danville, Illinois: Grace & Truth, 1990).
28. See Dronsfield, *The 'Brethren' since 1870.*

the group of the nineteen were excluded from the Alnwick assembly. In 1906, due to the state of division, the Brethren in Alnwick ceased to break bread together. Both sides appealed to neighbouring assemblies for recognition. One of these assemblies, Glanton, became involved in the issue, decided to view all regular activities in the neighbouring town as either having ceased or liable to do so, and welcomed the Alnwick Brethren to break bread in Glanton on an individual basis after examining each person's convictions. The Alnwick Brethren who had been received into the Glanton assembly were then sent back to Alnwick and declared part of the only 'regular' assembly there.

Twelve Glanton Brethren (while others disagreed) signed a 'Statement of Facts' justifying their actions. By 1907, the division had extended to the assemblies in Newcastle and Edinburgh. In 1908, the Brethren in Edinburgh who disagreed with how Glanton had handled the Alnwick incident withdrew from the local assembly and started meeting independently at 12 Merchiston Place. In August 1908, a sister from Merchiston Place arrived at Stoke Newington, one of the London assemblies, with a letter of recommendation, thus forcing the London Brethren to investigate the issue. The final, although not unanimous, decision was that the London assemblies would welcome the Edinburgh Brethren from Merchiston Place. This decision implied that Glanton's attitude had been objectionable.[29]

Brethren IV assemblies, most of those in Northumberland, plus a few abroad, including some in the United States, totalling 225 in all, supported Glanton, giving rise to a group known as the Glanton Brethren in Great Britain and later labelled as Brethren VI by the US Bureau of the Census. Many believers within this group were

29. Wellershaus, *Die Wahrheit Gottes*, 16–17.

not particularly concerned by the specifics of the Alnwick affair. Rather, the Alnwick incident was an opportunity for expressing their reserves about the teachings and leadership of Raven and his successor James Taylor Sr.

Brethren III followed the affair closely, hoping that those siding with Glanton would eventually join their group. However, several attempts to persuade Glanton Brethren, or Brethren VI, to join Brethren III failed, although links were established that were to be maintained over the following decades. From 1909 onwards, several Brethren VI Assemblies joined Grant's Brethren I. For fifty years, Brethren VI formed an interesting example of an independent group which was simultaneously tempted either to move towards the Open Brethren (II) or to attempt to reunite all the non-Open Brethren in one fold, whilst rejecting the authority of living teachers and therefore excluding Brethren IV.[30]

In 1938, a group known as Little Glanton split from Brethren VI, on the basis that the latter were becoming too close to the Open Brethren.[31] Some of these dissident assemblies remained autonomous, while others, especially in the United States, joined Brethren VIII, who had, as we have seen, left Grant's Brethren I for similar reasons. Finally, in 1974, Brethren VI's ties of friendship with Brethren III, which had been maintained for several decades, in England at least, came to bear fruit: the Glanton Brethren (VI) disappeared as an autonomous body, merging with Brethren III.

In 1908, Brethren III had another issue with a local assembly in Tunbridge Wells, Kent, the after-effects of which have persisted to this day. Once again, the casus belli appears to be trivial, as it involved the exclusion of a member who was accused of attending

---

30. George W. Ware, *Later Contentions for the Faith* (Guildford: G.W. Ware, 1931).
31. Ware, *Later Contentions for the Faith*, 31–32.

meetings too infrequently, but the real issue was the right of members of a local assembly to appeal to a higher authority in similar circumstances. Theoretically, all the groups descended from Darby were suspicious of authoritarianism and centralising authority in general. However, in practical terms, as they grew, they ended up accepting some structure and coordination above the local fellowships. Lowe took a stand against the Tunbridge Wells Brethren, who left, taking with them a significant number of assemblies under the banner of the independence of local fellowships.[32] This was an important split, which involved most Brethren III assemblies in the United States, where the 'Tunbridge Wells Brethren' were designated Brethren V in censuses, and a significant number in South Africa.

In 1940, this division was partially healed and all the English Brethren V, apart from a dozen assemblies, returned to the Brethren III fold. However, in the United States, Brethren V, while doctrinally very close to Brethren III, continued to have a separate existence. With the help of the Bible Truth Publishers company, which is very active in reprinting Darby's writings, they make up the best-known and perhaps largest non-Open Brethren group in the United States,[33] with some 180 assemblies and 10,000 members, a missionary activity covering many countries, and an internal history that has also witnessed several minor divisions.

In 1926, in the course of their attempts to unite all non-Open Brethren who were critical of Raven, Brethren III celebrated their merger with William Kelly's party. Kelly had died twenty years previously, and his faction, as we have seen, formed the English

---

32. Stanley Charles, *The Church of God* (St. Louis, Missouri: Bible Truth Publishers, 1982).
33. Piepkorn, 'Plymouth Brethren (Christian Brethren)', 179; Melton, *Melton's Encyclopedia of American Religions*, 8th ed., 529.

precursor, if not the actual root, of the American Brethren I. In 1953, Brethren III absorbed Brethren VII. They did the same with Brethren VIII in 1974, thereby completing the reunification of that part of the Brethren I tradition which had eschewed the drift towards the Open Brethren (II).

Brethren IX remained untouched by this major series of mergers, which led to Brethren III being known as the 'Reunited Brethren'. Dubbed the 'Ames Brethren' by Piepkorn in his four-category addition to the Bureau of the Census' existing six,[34] after their founder, Laurence W. Ames, Brethren IX split from Brethren VIII in 1949, distrustful of their discussions underway with a view to reuniting with other groups.[35] There are still several hundred Brethren IX in the United States and the Bahamas, with radio stations and magazines providing them a larger audience beyond their small number of members. However, they had a further division of their own in the New York area in 1973.

Brethren III can claim to have arrived, with all their mergers with other branches, at the end of a long path towards reunification. On the other end, divisions continue to occur. In France, there are in fact two different groups of Brethren III, with the very similar names of Assemblée des frères and Assemblée des frères darbystes. The second group remains closed to the international Brethren III, while the first originates from a schism which occurred in Marseille in 1997 among the followers of a popular local evangelist, who was disfellowshipped because of his use of modern techniques of communication and methods of evangelisation, which were not particularly appreciated by the more conservative local Brethren. Further doctrinal controversies in the year 2000 about how to interpret the

34. Piepkorn, 'Plymouth Brethren (Christian Brethren)', 170.
35. Hamilton Smith, *Perspectives on the True Church* (Minneapolis, Minnesota: Christian Literature, 1967).

principle of separation led to a division between the two groups, with the schismatic Assemblée des frères gathering some 60% of the existing French Brethren III. Because of this schism, Brethren III activities at the centre of Brus, in the village of Mars, in the area between Le Chambon sur Lignon and Saint-Agrève, in southern France, were discontinued. There, in 1969, an impressive hall with a capacity of 1,200 had been built and large meetings had been organised every year for Pentecost and around August 15. The nearby region has the largest density of Exclusive Brethren in France, including both Brethren III and Brethren IV. As the activities at the Brus centre have been resumed, a seasonal 'spiritual tourism' by Brethren III has developed in the summer in the area.[36]

Schisms are in a way unavoidable in a loosely organised network such as the Brethren III, which does not recognise any central authority. However, to claim that the 21st-century witnesses a 're-dividing' of the Reunited Brethren, as some do,[37] appears somewhat exaggerated. In 2003, Melton estimated Brethren III to have some 1,500 congregations worldwide.[38] In 2009, he mentioned 100 congregations in the United States and Canada and 'many hundreds' in other countries.[39] It is difficult to establish statistics with respect to their membership, but rumours of a decline in the number of members are now too widespread to be discounted. It may be that there are today in the world less than 100,000 Brethren III who see themselves as forming part of a single organisation, although, alongside the more 'institutional' forms, many autonomous assemblies and small groups also exist.

---

36. Christian Maillebouis, 'Sur l'implantation du 'darbysme' en France au XXe siècle', *Bulletin de la Société de l'histoire du protestantisme français* 159 (April–May–June 2013), 329–364.
37. Philip Nunn, *The Re-Dividing of the Reunited Brethren: An Attempt to Diagnose* (Quindio, Colombia: Armenia, 2003).
38. J. Gordon Melton, *Encyclopedia of American Religions*, 7th ed. (Detroit: Gale, 2003), 589.
39. Melton, *Melton's Encyclopedia of American Religions*, 8th ed., 526.

The doctrinal approach of Brethren III can be summarised by stating that they insist on salvation through grace and faith, the need for a genuine conversion and consistent walk with God, the return of the Lord to rapture the Church, formed of all true believers, and the gathering of Christians around the Lord without any other authority. Brethren III also insist on the priesthood of all believers without any official designations and thus on the freedom of each brother to take part actively in meetings, seeking guidance from the Holy Spirit. Brethren III remain strictly faithful to Darby and his grand scheme of dispensations into which history is divided, including the distinction between the 'Church of Christ' and the 'Church of men', the latter being seen as having been irretrievably corrupted since the end of the apostolic age. Since restoration of the Church of apostolic times is impossible by definition, small groups of believers, who have separated from the 'Church of men' and the world, wait confidently for the imminent second coming of the Lord.

Brethren III have also adopted Darby's ideas on the general apostasy of all institutional, hierarchically organised churches, and thus of the need to separate themselves both from religious systems and from believers who belong to them, choosing rather to unite with those who attempt to fulfil the principles of the universal Church locally. Today, this strict principle of 'separation', shared by Brethren III and IV, is still the principal distinctive feature of these Brethren. They regret the failure of other factions within the Brethren movement to separate from those who commit serious sins and do not repent adequately, and those who spread doctrines that they regard as being against biblical teaching.

Partaking of the Lord's Supper, which holds a central place and is celebrated every Sunday, is strictly reserved for Brethren who are members of the local fellowship, known as an assembly, and who are 'in fellowship' with one another. Brethren III do not practice infant baptism, although in some circumstances, and not without internal controversies, some congregations may recognise as valid the baptism administered in infancy, in other churches, to those who convert to their faith. Women do not teach or lead the prayer at meetings, during which they cover their heads with a veil. The principle according to which any decision taken by an assembly, particularly with respect to partaking of the Lord's Supper or exclusion from the latter, is deemed to be binding for all other assemblies anywhere else in the world, is seen as a means towards real unity of the body of Christ, although in the present state of Christianity Brethren III acknowledge that this unity cannot be fully achieved.

BRETHREN IV AND THEIR SCHISMS
(BRETHREN X)

I will present in Chapter 4 a study of the daily life in the Brethren IV community, known today as the Plymouth Brethren Christian Church, or the Exclusive Brethren (although the name 'Exclusive Brethren' is also used for Brethren III), and of its interaction with the larger society. Here, I situate Brethren IV within the map of the different Brethren fellowships. Brethren IV have as good grounds as anybody for claiming that they are the most direct continuation of the original Darbyites. As mentioned earlier, at the time of the 1890 separation, most Darbyite assemblies in Continental Europe fell in with those elders who were hostile to Raven, while the latter could count on the support of the historic assemblies in the city of London, those most directly connected to Darby. Although they hold many doctrines in common, and the same literature can often be found circulating within both groups, Brethren IV differ from Brethren III both theologically and sociologically. Theologically, Brethren IV acknowledge the importance of a recognised leader, to whom God entrusts the charge of guiding the fellowship. This idea is in direct opposition to Brethren II's principle that there should be no central authority guiding the Brethren. As for Brethren III, they agree that an 'authorised preacher' was entrusted by God with a special role, but this preacher was Darby only. For them, there is no living heir to Darby's historical role. Brethren III continue to be guided not by a living preacher, but by Darby's writings.

From a sociological point of view, Brethren IV gradually adopted measures that are even more stringent than those of Brethren III to guarantee their 'separation' from modernity, since they hold the modern world to be increasingly immoral and corrupt. Recognising a single international leader has led Brethren IV not only to accept Raven's ideas and those of his successors, even when they may appear to be new with respect to Darby's, but also to turn them into a membership test. Most of Raven's teachings were expressed in conversations, of which notes were taken by the Brethren, so that hasty or selective reading could easily result in misunderstandings or accusations of heresy. For instance, Raven was accused of diametrically opposed doctrinal deviations with respect to the nature of Jesus Christ,[40] and the debate on his writings is still ongoing.

Raven's successor, the Irishman James Taylor, known as Taylor Sr. to distinguish him from his son and successor also called James Taylor, expanded these doctrinal elaborations still further. In fifty years of ministry, he led hundreds of Bible meetings, whose notes were collected in 112 volumes, which some found difficult to

40. See Frederick Edward Raven, *Readings and Addresses in the United States* (Kingston-on-Thames: Stow Hill Bible and Tract Depot, 1902).

understand.[41] The two main doctrinal controversies in which he was involved concerned the title of Jesus Christ as the 'Son of God from all eternity' and the role of the Holy Spirit in prayer. In 1929, based on teachings he gleaned from Raven, Taylor Sr. put forward a doctrine according to which Jesus Christ was not the 'Son of God' from all eternity, but only took on this title at the time of the Incarnation. Between 1942 and 1949, Taylor Sr. also progressively introduced prayers and songs in which believers directly addressed the Holy Spirit, a practice that some critics considered as foreign to both the letter and the spirit of Darby's teachings.

What is certain is that Taylor Sr.'s writings were held to be normative by Brethren IV and that any practical or doctrinal departure from this line was grounds for eventual separation. This point is well illustrated by the Chinese incident of 1932–1935, at a time when, for a short period, Brethren IV seemed to have found a major opportunity for growth in China through their relationship with a charismatic local preacher, Watchman Nee (the nickname of Ni Shu-Tsu). Nee, an avid reader of Christian conservative theology, caught the attention of the Brethren IV in England by ordering books by Darby from one of their bookstores. A correspondence followed, and in 1930 an engineer and member of the Brethren IV who was travelling to China for business, Charles R. Barlow, visited Nee in Shanghai. This opened the way to a more formal meeting in 1932 between Nee and his associates and an official delegation of six men and two women from England, Australia, and the United States, dispatched to Shanghai by Brethren IV. They liked what they saw, and decided to break bread with the Chinese Brethren, although the latter made it clear that they had no desire to become part of a larger organisation.

---

41. See e.g., James Taylor, Sr., *Christ's Personal Service for the Saints* (Auckland, New Zealand: Bible and Gospel Trust, 1925).

Upon hearing the reports from China, Taylor Sr. wrote 'the news from China is affecting and leaves us in no doubt that the work is of God. But the responsibility attaching to it is grave and calls for the most serious consideration by all, so that the Lord may stand by it and shield it from the enemy.'[42]

In 1933, Nee was invited to visit England and the United States and to meet Taylor Sr. Brethren IV considered Nee as being in fellowship with them and bound by their rules, while the Chinese evangelist felt free, without advising his hosts, to visit also other Christian leaders with whom he had been in correspondence, including Theodore Austin-Sparks in England and Thornton Stearns in the United States. Neither man was a member of Brethren IV, yet Nee broke bread with both. Taylor Sr. discovered this while Nee was travelling back to China and wrote to the elders in Shanghai asking them to disfellowship the evangelist, mentioning also what he regarded as Nee's departures from Darbyism in matters of eschatology and the rapture. The leaders of the Shanghai group answered that the strict principle of separation maintained by Taylor Sr. was not biblical and that, although they greatly respected the Western Brethren (IV), they were 'unable to walk together' with them. Their cherished doctrine that only one assembly of Brethren should exist in each city in the world, no matter how large, also put them at odds with Taylor Sr.[43]

Nee spent twenty years in the prisons of Communist China between 1952 and 1972,[44] but his most gifted pupil, Witness Lee, turned the Local Church, which considers itself to be the direct heir

---

42. William Buntain, 'The Exclusive Brethren and the Local Churches in China', unpublished manuscript, 2016; James Taylor, Sr., *Letters of James Taylor*, 2 vol. (Kingston-on-Thames: Stow Hill Bible and Tract Depot, 1956), 1: 377.

43. Buntain, 'The Exclusive Brethren'.

44. Angus Ian Kinnear, *Against the Tide (The Story of Watchman Nee)* (Eastbourne, UK: Victory Press, 1973).

of Nee's ideas (though this is disputed by other believers), into a major international force and into an organisation in which traces of the teaching of Brethren IV remain clearly visible.[45]

Taylor Sr. died in 1953 and several years passed before his son, James Taylor Jr., was accepted as his successor by the large majority of Brethren IV, despite his father having clearly indicated him as such. Difficulties continued until the conference that took place in 1959 in the Methodist Central Hall in London, where the leadership of Taylor Jr. was recognised. His opponents eventually left Brethren IV and established their own meetings.

This very small minority group that left Brethren IV in 1959 has since become known as the 'Pre-Aberdeen Outs', to distinguish them from the 'Post-Aberdeen Outs', that is, those who fell out with Taylor Jr. shortly before the latter's death at the Aberdeen conference in 1970. During that conference, Taylor Jr., by that time old and exhausted (he died later that year), was accused not only of criticism some regarded as too harsh and abrasive against his opponents, but also of drinking alcohol in excess and of attitudes disrespectful of women. There is convincing evidence that the latter accusations were false and were made during a campaign aimed at destroying his authority by those critical of his leadership. Three authors of books echoing these accusations, including the well-known Dutch evangelical theologian Willem Johannes Ouweneel,[46]

---

45. See *The Beliefs and Practices of the Local Churches* (Anaheim, California: Living Stream Ministry, 1978); J. Gordon Melton, *An Open Letter Concerning the Local Church, Witness Lee and the God-Men Controversy* (Santa Barbara, California: Institute for the Study of American Religion, 1985).

46. Willem Johannes Ouweneel, *Het verhaal van de broeders. 150 jaar falen en genade*, 2 vol. (Aalten: Stichting Uit het Woord der Waarheid, 1976 and 1978). The other books were Norman Adams, *Goodbye, Beloved Brethren* (Aberdeen: Impulse Books, 1972), and Paul Thompson, with Tony Wailey and Trevor Lummis, *Living the Fishing* (London: Routledge and Kegan Paul, 1983), whose account of Taylor Jr. was largely derived from Adams.

Table 3.1 THE TEN MAIN GROUPINGS OF BRETHREN

Brethren I	Independent Brethren, mostly originating from William Kelly in England and Frederick W. Grant in the United States	Became extinct, after the Kelly party joined Brethren III in 1926 and most meetings of the Grant party joined Brethren II, while some joined Brethren III
Brethren II	Open Brethren, heirs of Müller-Groves in Britain and of Guicciardini and the Swiss Brethren in Continental Europe	Remain the largest group of Brethren worldwide, with more than one-and-a-half million members. The Needed Truth Brethren are their most significant schism
Brethren III	Exclusive Brethren who rejected Raven in 1890 (the 'Lowe Division') and the idea of a single authoritative leader for the worldwide movement	Known as the Lowe Brethren in the UK after William J. Lowe and as the Elberfeld Brethren in Germany after a conference held in that city in 1890. Absorbed the English branch of Brethren V, and Brethren VII and VIII, in a series of mergers to form a large group of Reunited Brethren numbering some 100,000 members (today in decline, and with local schisms in several countries). A significant schism is the 'Alte Elberfelder' Brethren in Germany

Table 3.1 CONTINUED

Brethren IV	Plymouth Brethren Christian Church: exclusive Brethren who accepted Raven and his various successors as recognised leaders	49,882 members worldwide (as of February 2017)
Brethren V	Born out of the dispute between Brethren III in Tunbridge Wells (Kent) in 1908 concerning issues of church government	In 1940, the English branch rejoined Brethren III; the American branch remained independent and spread to other countries (some 10,000 members today)
Brethren VI	'Glanton Brethren' who left Brethren IV in 1908 over issues relating to church government and leadership	In 1909, a moderate segment was absorbed into Brethren I; in 1938, a conservative split (Little Glanton Party) created independent fellowships, some of which later joined Brethren VIII. In 1974, Brethren VI merged into Brethren III
Brethren VII	Left Brethren I in 1928 over disciplinary and doctrinal issues	Merged into Brethren III in 1953

(continued)

Table 3.1 CONTINUED

Brethren VIII	Brethren I who refused to join the Open Brethren	After working together with Brethren VI, joined Brethren III in 1974 following several decades of negotiation
Brethren IX	'Ames Brethren' who left Brethren VIII in 1949, refusing to take part in discussions with a view to merging with other groups	Still have several hundred members in the US and the Bahamas; suffered the departure of a group of congregations in New York in 1973
Brethren X	Constellation of at least twenty main groups with no central coordination that, although generally accepting Raven's writings, left Brethren IV due to disagreements with his successors	Pre-Aberdeen Outs and Post-Aberdeen Outs are distinguished by their date of departure from Brethren IV—before or after an incident involving the leader of Brethren IV, James Taylor Jr., in Aberdeen in 1970. They have several thousand members, but are increasingly fragmented

publicly recanted their allegations. In 1990, court cases pending in the District Court of Utrecht and the Court of Appeal of Amsterdam against Ouweneel and his publisher were settled, with the Dutch theologian recognising as reliable a number of documents and witness testimonies showing that the accusations against Taylor Jr. had been fabricated by his opponents.[47]

However, some believed these accusations, and thus was born the 'post-Aberdeen' Brethren X split. Other controversies involved Taylor's successors, firstly the American farmer James Harvey Symington, and secondly two Australian businessmen, John Stephen Hales and his son Bruce David Hales. These controversies relate to general societal issues concerning Brethren IV and, as such, are discussed in the next chapter.

Piepkorn gathered all these dissidents under the 'Brethren X' label.[48] In fact, Brethren X are not a single fellowship but a galaxy of independent communities whose sole point in common is their opposition to Taylor Jr. and his successors. They have not been admitted into fellowship by Brethren III, because they retain confidence in the writings of Raven and Taylor Sr., which Brethren III believe to be unorthodox.

There are several thousand Brethren X throughout the world. Brethren IV, who today prefer to be identified as members of the Plymouth Brethren Christian Church, have a total of 49,882 members according to their very precise statistics updated to February 2017, with the larger communities in Australia, the United Kingdom, United States, New Zealand, and Canada, and an old and established presence in the Caribbean, Argentina, France, Germany, Sweden, Italy, Switzerland, Ireland, the Netherlands, and Denmark. See Table 3.1 for a summary of the differences between the ten main groupings of Brethren.

---

47. A copy of the settlement document of April 1990 is in the archives of CESNUR (Center for Studies on New Religions), Torino, Italy.
48. Piepkorn, 'Plymouth Brethren (Christian Brethren)', 170.

4

Retrenchment and Mainstreaming

The Plymouth Brethren Christian Church in the 21st Century

THE BRITISH CHARITY COMMISSION CASE (2006–2014)

In 2006, Britain amended its 1960 Charities Act, removing the centuries-old presumption that organisations involved in religious activities, education, or poverty relief should automatically be considered as operating for the public benefit. The 2006 legislation, however, did not clearly spell out what constituted 'public benefit' and left it to the Charity Commission and eventually to the courts to decide.

Brethren III and IV had their problems with the Charity Commission before 2006,[1] but in general managed to have their organisations registered, and thus entitled to tax exemptions. Things changed in 2006. Public benefit had now to be proved. Additionally, conservative Christian groups felt that the political and cultural context was now somewhat hostile. They claimed that, although

---

1. See Bryan R. Wilson, 'A Sect at Law', *Encounter* 60, 1 (January 1983): 81–87.

some fundamentalist Muslim bodies were scrutinised more deeply after terrorist attacks, non-Christian organisation such as the neo-pagan Druid Network, registered in 2010, were treated with more leniency by the Charity Commission.

The latter advised Brethren IV that there might be a problem, as the Brethren seemed to operate mostly for the benefit of their members rather than society at large. Conversations followed, and the Charity Commission and Brethren IV agreed that a test case should be created. In 2009, Preston Down Trust (PDT), which operated a Brethren IV hall in Torbay, Devon, applied for registration with the Charity Commission. After several meetings, the Commission informed PDT in 2011 that it was considering seeking the advice of the independent Charity Tribunal. In 2012, however, the Commission rejected PDT's application without having sought the Tribunal's advice.

Preston Down Trust appealed to the Charity Tribunal and, while the case was proceeding, several British religious organisations, although theologically distant from Brethren IV, realised that allowing the Commission to define 'public benefit' by considering the doctrines of a group was potentially dangerous for the religious liberty of many denominations. Members of Parliament took an interest in the issue, protesting the Commission's attitude, and proceedings were suspended in 2013, allowing the parties to negotiate again. In 2014, a settlement was finally reached. Brethren IV agreed to introduce in their statutes two schedules entitled *Statements of Core Doctrine* and *Faith in Practice*. The first clarified fourteen fundamental beliefs. The second set out how these beliefs should work in practice and covered inter alia separation, protection from unduly harsh decisions of internal judicial bodies, and a compassionate treatment of those wishing to leave the

Brethren. The Commission then registered PDT as a charity.[2] On 15 February 2016, the Commission released the report of an investigation aimed at ascertaining whether Brethren IV were complying with the terms of the 2014 agreement and concluded that they indeed did.[3]

British Brethren IV saw these proceedings as a matter of life and death. Without charitable status, there was the risk that their places of worship might be confiscated, depriving the Brethren both of assets worth millions of pounds and of places where to hold their meetings. Brethren IV spent over one million pounds, raised among their members, in legal expenses. They also realised that, without the bipartisan intervention of several members of the British Parliament in their favour, the Charity Commission might never had accepted to settle.

The whole Charity Commission saga created in many Brethren an awareness that they had made powerful enemies. They were accustomed to accusations of heresy by other Christians. What was new and disturbing was that media and organisations connected with the so-called anti-cult movement were branding them as a 'cult' harmful to families and children because of their way of living, quite irrespective from their theological doctrines. This was new for many Brethren, both in Britain and internationally, as they firmly believed that their fellowships were a safe haven protecting children from an increasingly difficult and immoral external world. It was perhaps less new for their Australian Brethren, as the local media and anti-cultists had started similar campaigns against Brethren IV there since the last decade of

2. Charity Commission for England and Wales, *Preston Down Trust: Decision of the Commission* (London: Charity Commission for England and Wales, 2014).
3. Charity Commission for England and Wales, *Case Report Preston Down Trust (1155382)* (London: Charity Commission for England and Wales, 2016).

the 20th century.[4] In fact, Brethren III were potentially open to similar criticism, as they shared several practices with Brethren IV. However, the existence of a clear structure within Brethren IV, with a leader whose statements might be identified as normative, and criticised as such, made them a somewhat easier target.

While sectarian criticism remained confined to the circles of those interested in religious disputes, secular accusations of creating harm for children and families influenced governmental agencies. The problem did not concern Britain only. In Australia, labelling the Plymouth Brethren as a 'cult' was an exercise in which journalist Michael Bachelard specialised in such an obsessive way that his newspaper, *The Age*, ended up being sued in 2016 by Brethren IV, a group normally very reluctant to engage in litigations.[5] In 2014, in the Canadian province of Manitoba, the *Winnipeg Free Press* started a major campaign against Brethren IV largely based on Bachelard, although they also mentioned shortly the different opinions of academics such as Eileen Barker.[6] In Australia, anti-cult campaigns against Brethren IV threatened the public funding of their schools, within a political context where state support to religious schools in general was questioned.[7]

4. Bernard Doherty, 'Quirky Neighbors or the Cult Next-Door? An Analysis of Public Perceptions of the Exclusive Brethren in Australia', *International Journal for the Study of New Religions* 3, 2 (2012): 163–211; Bernard Doherty, 'The 'Brethren Cult Controversy': Dissecting a Contemporary Australian 'Social Problem'', *Alternative Spirituality and Religion Review* 4, 1 (2013): 25–48.

5. Michael Bachelard, *Behind the Exclusive Brethren: Politics Persuasion and Persecution* (Melbourne: Scribe Publications, 2008); Chris Merritt, 'The Age Sued for Brethren Article', *The Australian*, 18 July 2016.

6. Bill Redekop, 'The Closed-Door Church: Inside the Secretive and Strict Plymouth Brethren Sect in Manitoba', *Winnipeg Free Press*, 5 October 2014, available at http://www.winnipegfreepress.com/local/The-closed-door-church-258336281.html, last accessed 11 August 2016.

7. Marian Maddox, 'The Church, the State and the Classroom: Questions Posed by an Overlooked Sector in Australia's Education Market', *University of New South Wales Law Journal* 34, 1 (2011): 300–315; Marian Maddox, *Taking God to School: The End of Australia's Egalitarian Education?* (Crows Nest, New South Wales: Allen & Unwin, 2014), 81–86.

A similar hostile attention targeted the Brethren IV school in Nyby, Sweden.[8] In France, the anti-cult movement is particularly strong, and the government has a special agency aimed at controlling 'cults', the MIVILUDES, Mission interministérielle de vigilance et de lutte contre les dérives sectaires (Inter-ministerial Mission for Monitoring and Combating Cultic Deviances). A handful of individuals created in 2003 in Saint-Etienne an anti-Brethren association called Association nationale d'aide aux victimes des Frères exclusifs (National Association for Helping the Victims of Exclusive Brethren). It was never very active but caught the attention of MIVILUDES, which mentioned the Brethren in a 2006 report on 'cults' potentially harmful to children.[9] In 2014, the French MP Rudy Salles introduced a report at the Council of Europe where he offered the Brethren IV schools, singling out the one in Sweden, as an example that 'cults' were guilty of 'psychological abuse' of minors.[10] Ultimately, however, the Salles report was voted down by the Parliamentary Assembly of the Council of Europe.

The Brethren were both disturbed and offended by these attacks. In retrospect, however, they derived from them two unexpected, and certainly unintended, benefits. First, at least Brethren IV, whose structure allowed for an organised response, felt compelled to answer the criticism. In the process, they could explain to outsiders a few recent

---

8. See Liselotte Frisk and Sanja Nilsson, 'Uppväxt och skolgång för barnen inom Kristna Kyrkan Plymouthbröderna: det svenska Perspektivet', in *Guds nya barnbarn: Att växa upp i kontroversiella religiösa grupper*, ed. Liselotte Frisk, Sanja Nilsson, and Peter Åkerbäck (Stockholm: Dialogos, 2017), 238–271; and Liselotte Frisk and Sanja Nilsson, 'Raising and Schooling Children in the Plymouth Brethren Christian Church: The Swedish Perspective', in *Children in Minority Religions: Growing Up in Controversial Religious Groups*, ed. Liselotte Frisk, Sanja Nilsson, and Peter Åkerbäck (Sheffield, UK, and Bristol, Connecticut: Equinox, 2018), 333–361.

9. MIVILUDES (Mission interministérielle de vigilance et de lutte contre les dérives sectaires), *Rapport au Premier ministre Année 2005* (Paris: MIVILUDES, 2006), 16, 18, and 24.

10. Rudy Salles, *The Protection of Minors Against Excesses of Sects: Report* (Strasbourg: Council of Europe, Parliamentary Assembly, Committee on Legal Affairs and Human Rights, 2014).

changes in their organisation, pointing out that criticism in the 21st century largely relied on events of the 1960s, 1970s, and 1980s. The objection that changes came precisely in response to anti-cult criticism and the Charity Commission controversy is not supported by chronology. The first reforms were introduced much earlier.[11]

Second, social scientists who were familiar with the anti-cult movement started taking a renewed interest in the Brethren. Unlike most Brethren leaders, they had a long knowledge of how anti-cultists operated, had developed a criticism of the anti-cult movement since at least the 1980s, and were quickly able to understand its strategy towards the Brethren. And, unlike the anti-cultists, academic scholars could interpret what was going on among Brethren IV by using the sociological models of mainstreaming and retrenchment discussed in Chapter 1 of this book.

Comprehensive studies of Brethren IV started being produced by social scientists in different continents. Bernard Doherty studied the Brethren and their opponents in Australia and beyond.[12] Liselotte Frisk and Sanja Nilsson conducted a field study of children and schooling among the Swedish Brethren.[13] I studied Brethren IV schools and visited them in Italy, the United States, Sweden, and

---

11. See Bernard Doherty, 'The Brethren Movement: From Itinerant Evangelicals to Introverted Sectarians', in *Handbook of Global Contemporary Christianity: Movements, Institutions, and Allegiance*, ed. Stephen Hunt (Leiden: Brill, 2016), 357–381.

12. Doherty, 'Quirky Neighbors or the Cult Next-Door?'; Doherty, 'The "Brethren Cult Controversy"'; Bernard Doherty, '"The Nurture and Admonition of the Lord": Brethren Schooling and the Debate on Religious Schools in Australia', paper presented at the 2015 annual conference of CESNUR (Center for Studies on New Religions), Tallinn, Estonia, 17–20 June 2015, available at http://www.cesnur.org/2015/doherty_brethren_tallinn_2015. pdf, last accessed 11 August 2016; Doherty, 'The Brethren Movement'; Bernard Doherty and Laura Dyason, 'Revision or Re-Branding? The Plymouth Brethren Christian Church in Australia under Bruce D. Hales 2002–2016', in *Radical Changes in Minority Religions*, ed. Eileen Barker and Beth Singler (Abingdon, UK, and New York: Routledge, forthcoming [2018]).

13. Frisk and Nilsson, 'Raising and Schooling Children'.

France, interviewing teachers and pupils.[14] Other studies, including doctoral dissertations, are forthcoming. These studies have been able to clarify several controversial issues, particularly in the fields of the use of the label 'cult', separatism, education and schools, and the elusive 'public benefit.'

BRETHREN IV AND THE QUESTION OF CULTS

Among the most studied topics in the social scientific study of religious movements are the so-called cult wars of the 1970s and 1980s.[15] In the period from the late 1960s to the early 1970s, dozens of new religious movements appeared in the United States and in Europe, some originating from Asia. Many of these movements targeted college students, leading some to drop out of school and become full-time missionaries, throwing their families into shock. While some of the converts' parents were not religious, others found the religious reaction to the phenomenon to be weak and inadequate. Most religious organisations limited themselves to a theological critique and to the labelling of the movements as 'heretical'. Thus, next to an old religious 'counter-cult' movement, a similar,

---

14. Massimo Introvigne, 'Who Is Afraid of the Plymouth Brethren? Brethren Controversies in Historical Perspective', paper presented at the 2015 annual conference of CESNUR (Center for Studies on New Religions), Tallinn, Estonia, 17–20 June 2015, available at http://www.cesnur.org/2015/Brethren2015.pdf, last accessed 11 August 2016.

15. Anson D. Shupe, Jr. and David Bromley, *The New Vigilantes: Deprogrammers, Anti-Cultists, and the New Religions* (Beverly Hills, California, and London: Sage, 1980); David G. Bromley and Anson D. Shupe, Jr., *Strange Gods: The Great American Cult Scare* (Boston: Beacon Press, 1981); Anson D. Shupe, Jr. and David Bromley, eds., *Anti-Cult Movements in Cross-Cultural Perspective* (New York and London: Garland, 1994); Eugene V. Gallagher, ed., *'Cult Wars' in Historical Perspective: New and Minority Religions* (Abingdon and New York: Routledge, 2016).

but secular, 'anti-cult' movement appeared.[16] The secular movement claimed not to be interested in creeds, but only in deeds, wanting to scrutinise the new movements from a non-religious perspective and to take some sort of action to save the 'victims' from the 'cults'.

We shall not retrace the full path of the anti-cult movement here. Suffice it to note that in the United States in the 1970s, and contemporaneously in Europe, in France especially, the anti-cult movement became 'professional', moving from an early stage, when it was led by the parents of cult members, to a new stage dominated by psychologists and attorneys. In this new phase, there was a merging of the ideas and slogans about the harmfulness of 'cults' in general and the body of theories connected to brainwashing.

'Brainwashing' was a concept originally developed during the Cold War to explain why apparently 'normal' people could convert to such an evil ideology as communism. The brainwashing theory that was applied to the cults by the anti-cult movement in the 1970s and 1980s was for the most part a construction of Margaret Thaler Singer, a clinical psychologist who lectured at the University of California, Berkeley. Singer prepared a list of criteria to distinguish 'cults from legitimate religions,[17] which was widely criticised by academic scholars of new religious movements. The latter, in their large majority, also believed that brainwashing theories lacked any empirical evidence and were being used as a way of discriminating against unpopular religions.[18] They also criticised the anti-cultists' reliance on 'apostates', that is, former members

---

16. Massimo Introvigne, 'The Secular Anti-Cult and the Religious Counter-Cult Movement: Strange Bedfellows or Future Enemies?' in *New Religions and the New Europe*, ed. Eric Towler (Aarhus, Oxford and Oakville, Connecticut: Aarhus University Press, 1995), 32–54.

17. Margaret Thaler Singer and Janja Lalich, *Cults in Our Midst* (San Francisco: Jossey-Bass, 1995).

18. See Dick Anthony and Massimo Introvigne, *Le Lavage de cerveau: mythe ou réalité?* (Paris: L'Harmattan, 2006).

who militantly denounced the 'cults' they had left, observing that only a tiny minority of ex-members of religious movements became 'apostates'. There was no reason to regard apostates as more reliable than both actual members and the majority of ex-members who did not express animosity against the group they once belonged to.[19]

After several years of legal battles, the *Fishman* decision of the US District Court for the Northern District of California in 1990 excluded Singer's testimony, noting that 'theories regarding the coercive persuasion practiced by religious cults are not sufficiently established to be admitted as evidence in federal courts of law.'[20] Most courts followed the *Fishman* ruling, causing a deep crisis in the American anti-cult movement,[21] although in Europe anti-cultists still enjoyed the support of several government and inspired official policies. Brainwashing theories and the Singer definition of 'cults' became, however, widely discredited among academics, although they remained popular in certain sectors of the media.

The crisis of the anti-cult movement was made worse by two other factors. First, the increasing concern about terrorism diverted public resources in several countries from combating cults to combating radicalisation among Islamic immigrants. Second, the main targets of the anti-cult movements either declined and became less visible, as it happened in the cases of The Family (formerly called the Children of God) and the Unification Church, or proved

---

19. See David G. Bromley, ed., *Falling from the Faith: Causes and Consequences of Religious Apostasy* (Newbury Park and Beverly Hills, California: Sage, 1988); David G. Bromley, ed., *The Politics of Religious Apostasy: The Role of Apostates in the Transformation of Religious Movements* (Westport, Connecticut, and London: Praeger, 1998).

20. US District Court for the Northern District of California, 'Opinion (Jensen J.). Case No. CR-88-0616 DLJ. United States v. Steven Fishman', 13 April 1990, 743 F. *Supp.* 713, 14.

21. See James T. Richardson, 'Sociology and the New Religions: "Brainwashing" the Courts, and Religious Freedom', in *Witnessing for Sociology: Sociologists in Court*, ed. Pamela Jenkins and Steve Kroll-Smith (Westport, Connecticut, and London: Praeger, 1996), 115–137.

very capable of resisting in court both governmental and anti-cult attacks, as was the case for the Church of Scientology.

As old targets either proved formidable opponents in court or became less newsworthy because of their reduced visibility, the anti-cult movement needed new targets to prove its continuing relevance. It found a treasure chest in the long lists of 'heretics', including the Exclusive Brethren, prepared by evangelical counter-cultists, and quickly extended to them the accusations of brainwashing.

Anti-cultists also realised that there was a widespread moral panic about the idea that children were abused, manipulated, and unduly indoctrinated by religious groups. By definition, moral panics do start from real problems, but amplify and exaggerate their prevalence. There is a serious problem of child abuse in several religious organisations. Anti-cultists, however, mistakenly claimed that the problem was more prevalent in 'cults' than in mainline religions. Sociological and criminological studies proved that the opposite was the case. There were more cases of sexual abuse and paedophilia among the clergy and pastors of large organisations, including the Catholic Church and several large Protestant denominations, than in the new religious movements.[22] Finally, the struggling anti-cult movement also increasingly tried to find allies in other advocacy organisations. It was happy to targets cults it can accuse of homophobia, political activism, and support of right-wing candidates, allegedly violating the principle of Church-State separation because this could mobilise liberal political groups and gay activists.

Exclusive Brethren were always a target of the Christian counter-cult movement, for reasons dating back to Darby himself. However, anti-Brethren publications found a limited audience outside the

---

22. See Anson D. Shupe, Jr., *In the Name of All That's Holy: A Theory of Clergy Malfeasance* (Westport, Connecticut, and London: Praeger, 1995).

specialised milieu of evangelical apologetics. Anti-cultists' interest in the Brethren was comparatively recent and was born from specific weaknesses and problems in the anti-cult movement. It needed to expand its list of targets and found Brethren IV as a group that both was historically targeted by evangelical counter-cultists and had its share of ex-members who published lurid accounts of their life in the movement, most of them written many years after they had left the Brethren.[23] The fact that Brethren IV operated a highly visible network of schools maintaining traditional Christian values allowed anti-cultists to claim that they were 'manipulating' or 'psychologically abusing' children. Separatism was used as evidence that Brethren IV were creating a totalitarian environment, thus favourable to 'mind control'.

Anti-cultists also tried to gather the support of politically liberal and gay activists by claiming that in Australia and New Zealand, and perhaps elsewhere, Brethren IV tried to influence elections and interacted with conservative politicians, particularly after Bruce Hales became the international leader in 2002. Brethren IV do not vote nor run for office. They maintain that, in general, governments should be respected as appointed by God, based on the words of the Pauline Letters to the Romans, 13:1. Brethren IV, however, have regarded it as a duty to 'testify' to members of the governments and of parliaments concerning not only issues that affect them but also matters of general interest for the moral prosperity of their countries. This happened very openly during the Charity Commission case in Britain, and in Australia when laws hostile to religious schools were discussed.

---

23. See e.g., Ngaire Ruth Thomas, *Behind Closed Doors: A Startling Story of Exclusive Brethren Life* (Auckland: Random House New Zealand, 2005); David Tchappat, *Breakout: How I Escaped from the Exclusive Brethren* (Chatswood, New South Wales: New Holland Australia, 2009); Joy Nason, *Joy & Sorrow: The Story of an Exclusive Brethren Survivor* (Sydney: Centennial, 2015); Rebecca Stott, *In the Days of Rain* (London: 4th Estate, 2017).

Opponents, however, claimed that Brethren IV did much more and supported conservative candidates whose positions they shared on family-related issues, including opposition to same-sex marriage, during general political elections in Australia and New Zealand. Anti-cultists claimed that this was a strategy personally coordinated by Bruce Hales and faithfully implemented by the Brethren. Doherty notes that evidence for these accusations is scarce. It is true that individual Brethren, acting on their own initiative, felt it was their duty to express their positions on certain sensitive issues through pamphlets and articles, and some Brethren-owned businesses contributed funds, at least indirectly, to political campaigns. There was, however, no evidence that these activities were coordinated by the movement; rather, they were carried out on an individual basis.[24]

Are Brethren IV part of a 'cult'? On the one hand, the question does not make sense, if one follows the opinion, prevailing among scholars of new religious movements, that 'cult' is not a descriptive label with an empirically verifiable content but a political tool used by the adversaries of certain groups. On the other hand, media continue to use the word 'cult' and many in the general public are persuaded that 'cults' are something different from genuine religions, and something dangerous. It would, thus, be useful to add, that even if one would accept Singer's controversial criteria for distinguishing cults from bona fide religions, they would hardly apply to Brethren IV. Cults' trademark feature, for Singer, is that they try to convert potential new members through high-pressure, manipulative and often 'deceptive and indirect methods of persuasion and control' (Singer was the chair of the DIMPAC committee, whose report was ultimately rejected by the American Psychological

24. Doherty and Dyason, 'Revision or Re-Branding?'

Association).[25] Brethren IV are almost as far away as possible from the Unification Church or the Church of Scientology, which Singer regarded as the most typical examples of DIMPAC. Not only do Brethren IV use old, 19th-century style evangelism, but they certainly also do not measure their success in terms of new converts. In fact, they have even been described as 'a group which does not actively recruit members and relies almost solely on current members having large families to ensure the continuation and growth of the group'.[26] Their marginal growth is mostly due to their remarkable capacity to retain their young men and women in the movement, where they marry and have children. In this sense, they are not a cult according to the Singer DIMPAC model, quite irrespective from whether one accepts the model. Other accusations by the anti-cult movement are discussed in the following sections.

BRETHREN'S SEPARATISM: BETWEEN RETRENCHMENT AND MAINSTREAMING

Relying on theories advanced by psychiatrist Robert Jay Lifton about mind control in communist China,[27] anti-cultists claimed that 'brainwashing' requires a 'totalistic' environment to succeed. Opponents of Brethren IV argued that the principle of separation creates such a 'totalistic' situation. As Shuff demonstrated,

25. DIMPAC (American Psychological Association Task Force on Deceptive and Indirect Techniques of Persuasion and Control), *Report of the APA Task Force on Deceptive and Indirect Techniques of Persuasion and Control*, 1986, available at http://www.cesnur.org/testi/DIMPAC.htm, last accessed 11 August 2016; Massimo Introvigne, 'Advocacy, Brainwashing Theories, and New Religious Movements', *Religion*, 44, 2 (2014): 303–319.
26. Doherty and Dyason, 'Revision or Re-Branding?'
27. Robert Jay Lifton, *Thought Reform and the Psychology of Totalism: A Study of 'Brainwashing' in China* (New York: Norton, 1961).

separation has been interpreted in different ways in different times during the history of Brethren IV.[28] An initial tension existed between the principle that Brethren assemblies should unite all sincere believers in Christ and the idea that the churches represented Babylon, and Brethren should not associate with them. In the mature phase of his thought, Darby advocated and practiced both primary and secondary separation, that is, he asked his followers not to break bread not only with members of 'apostate' churches and heretics, but also with Christians who, although personally irreproachable in their doctrines and conduct, nonetheless associated with those who preached false doctrine or remained in the old religious organisations.

But the principle was continuously subject to different interpretations.[29] Later, the principles of primary and secondary separation prevailed. Taylor Sr. applied the doctrine rigidly, although he also maintained that the refusal of breaking bread should not imply that Brethren IV should not interact with other Christians in both their private and professional life. How, otherwise, could the Gospel be announced to non-Brethren?[30]

Shuff reconstructed this evolution by examining the theological principles guiding the different positions. There is, however, also a sociological context worth considering. As mentioned in our first chapter, Brethren IV occupy the fundamentalist niche. To their centre is the conservative niche, where Brethren II are located. Further away from the centre is the ultra-fundamentalist niche. As Buntain illustrates in his study of the Chinese incident of 1935, Brethren

---

28. Roger N. Shuff, 'From Open to Closed: A Study of the Development of Exclusivism within the Brethren Movement in Britain 1828–1953' (BD diss., University of Wales, 1996); Shuff, 'Open to Closed'; Roger N. Shuff, *Searching for the True Church: Brethren and Evangelicals in Mid-Twentieth-Century England* (Bletchley and Milton Keynes: Paternoster Press, 2005).

29. See Shuff, 'Open to Closed', 16.

30. Shuff, 'Open to Closed'. 31.

IV in the time of Taylor Sr. were well aware of a centripetal force attracting their members to Brethren II. They were very concerned about the attraction of Open Brethrenism, the more so because of the considerable missionary success of Brethren II. If anything, the Chinese episode, as they interpreted it, confirmed to them that the risk was very real.[31]

Reactions to centripetal forces in the more conservative niches take the shape of retrenchment. Affirming emphatically secondary separation, as Taylor Sr. did in the case of Watchman Nee, was a form of retrenchment. Although aware of the risk that separation might hinder evangelisation, Taylor Sr. regarded the possibility of slipping towards the Open Brethren as more dangerous.[32] Again, the process was not univocal. Some congregations applied the principles of separation in a more relaxed way, thus generating the impression in some of the leaders that the risk of Open Brethrenism was still very much more present. This prepared a new retrenchment in the years of Taylor Jr.

By interpreting certain texts of Raven, he asked the Brethren not only to avoid breaking bread with persons outside their fellowship and those who associated with them, but also to refrain from sharing a common meal such as a breakfast, lunch, or dinner with these persons. 'Common meal' refers to the social eating of a meal, involving fellowship, as distinct from routine drinks during the course of business, or meals served in hospitals, schools, or an aircraft or train.

Brethren IV should also not be 'linked together in association' with 'unbelievers'. Taylor Jr. interpreted Saint Paul's admonitions in 2 Timothy 2:19 and 2 Corinthians 6:14–18 that Christians should 'withdraw from iniquity' and 'come out from the midst of

---

31. Buntain, 'The Exclusive Brethren'.
32. Shuff, 'Open to Closed', 20–21.

them [unbelievers] and be separated', to the effect that, for example, Brethren should be part of a professional association, or corporate directorship, only with those who broke bread with them at the Lord's Supper. Taylor Sr. had already advised against marriages with non-Brethren and listening to the radio; his son added television. The prohibitions were not uniformly enforced everywhere,[33] but clearly a strong process of retrenchment and boundary maintenance was being promoted by the leadership.

In fundamentalist groups, retrenchment protects from centripetal impulses towards the mainstream yet involves the opposite risk of centrifugal movements towards isolation. These risks were noted by sociologists such as Wilson in his observation of the Brethren during the era of Taylor Jr.[34] That the risks were not purely theoretical was confirmed by the increasing facility of incurring excommunication, or being 'withdrawn from' during the Taylor Jr. era. Since meals were not to be shared with those 'withdrawn from' obvious problems were created for spouses and relatives. This situation continued with Taylor Jr.'s successor, Symington, who at the time also extended his predecessor's objections against digital technology, which was becoming more widely available to the public.

Excessive retrenchment either leads fundamentalist groups into ultra-fundamentalism (and decline) or generates an internal reaction in the form of mainstreaming. To a certain extent, the leadership itself may recognise the dangers of the centrifugal derive and promote a cautious centripetal process. This is what happened within Brethren IV when Bruce Hales succeeded his father in 2002 as international leader. He quickly recognised that, in the previous decades, misinterpretation of principles resulted in excommunication being

---

33. Shuff, 'Open to Closed'; Doherty and Dyason, 'Revision or Re-Branding?'
34. Wilson, 'The Exclusive Brethren'.

used too quickly, including 'for minor offences' and 'without sufficient patience and attempts at restoration before taking extreme action'.[35] In 2003, an initiative known as 'The Review' was started, reviewing past excommunications and offering apologies to those who appeared to have been excluded from fellowship on faulty or insufficient grounds. This preparedness to confront past shortcomings was widely recognised and commended, even by opponents, and a small but significant number of those approached took the opportunity to return to the Brethren.[36]

At the beginning of his tenure, Hales Jr. maintained his predecessors' concerns about digital technology, especially because of the widespread presence of pornography in the Internet.[37] Eventually, however, the attitude towards the Internet was revised, considering that filters against pornography and other content regarded as unhealthy were available. Brethren IV maintain certain cautions and limitations when using both computers and mobile phones. A Brethren-operated company, Universal Business Team, headquartered in Meadowbank, New South Wales, Australia, developed one of the world's leading suite of Internet management tools allowing filtering of contents deemed to be harmful for both children and adults.

THE QUESTION OF YOUTH

Brethren IV are a family-oriented community, and they emphasise the sacredness of marriage. Divorce is not excluded but is much rarer

35. Plymouth Brethren Christian Church, *Progression and Principles: The Plymouth Brethren Christian Church Today* (Chessington, UK: Plymouth Brethren Christian Church, 2014), 4.
36. See Doherty and Dyason, 'Revision or Re-Branding?'
37. Laura Dyason and Bernard Doherty, 'The Modern Hydra: The Exclusive Brethren's Online Critics', *St. Mark's Review* 233 (2015): 116–134.

than in the larger Western societies.[38] One of their most heartfelt concerns is to guarantee an adequate education to their children, while preserving them from the influence of the 'corrupt' external world. Children are baptised within the first weeks from their birth, which, not surprisingly, is criticised by those Protestant groups that regard infant baptism as unbiblical. They are regarded very early as members of the community and allowed, but not compelled to, participate in the daily prayer meetings and in the Sunday services, led by men with women in charge of the songs. Observation by Frisk and Nilsson, as well as by me, showed that most young boys and girls enjoy participating in the meetings, where they are together with their friends, and consider it a punishment not to be taken there by their parents.[39]

Young Brethren are taught an ethics of service since their early years. The study by Frisk and Nilsson in Sweden reported that 'children are taught to help other people and be towards others as you would like them to be towards you. Peter, for example, cuts grass for elderly in the congregation in his free time … Helena, a parent in the congregation, opened her home for an elderly member after an operation, and cared for her for several weeks' with the help of her children. The Swedish study also found that Brethren teenagers are 'well informed about what happens in the world'. Although they avoid books and articles with 'inappropriate content', most of them read daily newspapers regularly and are not less conversant with main world events than youth of different religious persuasions.

The same research also noticed that Brethren parents prefer to use rewards rather than punish their children: 'punishments do not

---

38. Norman Doe, 'The Plymouth Brethren Christian Church: A Comparative Appraisal of Its Regulatory Framework' (unpublished manuscript, 2013), 47–48.
39. Frisk and Nilsson, 'Raising and Schooling Children,' 339–340.

seem to be much used.' Finally, the Swedish scholars noted that a distinctive feature of the Brethren is 'the close relationship between parents and children. Parents emphasise the importance of keeping the family together and spending as much time as possible with their children. The whole family, or several families, often spend time with outdoor activities. Parents emphasise the importance of love and consideration.'[40]

Separation does not mean that older children cannot attend public schools where no Brethren alternatives exist, and all Brethren schools have non-Brethren teachers and principals. In 2015, I visited the Pascack Valley Campus, in upstate New York, that, besides having the peculiarity of being a Cold War military facility converted into a school by the Brethren, has a Roman Catholic woman as its principal. She seemed to be well liked by the students and very much at ease with them. Only, she (and I) ate separately from the Brethren students at lunch.

Brethren children are noticeable when they attend public schools because of their conservative dressing, with girls invariably wearing skirts. Schoolmates are understandably surprised that they do not watch television, listen to the radio, or go to movie theatres, although they watch movies regarded as not morally objectionable at home and do have some limited and supervised access to the Internet. Taylor Jr. enacted prohibitions against pets that are still followed with respects to cats and dogs, although some children do keep small animals such as birds.

On the other hand, Brethren IV teenagers are on average well-travelled. Visiting other Brethren communities is encouraged, and from Europe many went as far as Australia and United States, and vice versa. They report their excitement in travelling to faraway

40. Frisk and Nilsson, 'Raising and Schooling Children,' 337–357.

places and finding everywhere a place to stay, in the home of fellow Brethren. It is quite remarkable that members, in whatever country they are found, follow the same standards of dress and conduct, and the same procedure in their church services, which are invariably conducted in English. This global uniformity today is hardly found in any other body of Christians. Even at the local level, the practice of 'interchange', introduced by Symington, puts nearby communities in frequent contact with one another.

Some had the experience of moving from large cities to rural areas. Although Brethren IV did so for building up smaller assemblies and 'spreading the testimony' to new areas, moving to the countryside had several economic and social effects, discussed in 2001 by sociologist Matthew Tonts in his study of the rural community of Dalwallinu, in Western Australia,[41] where 182 Brethren IV settled between 1986 and 1996 in a village with a population of 697, plus 1,002 in the surrounding rural area. In Dalwallinu, Tonts noted, there was 'a widespread recognition that the Brethren have created significant local economic and employment benefits, and have contributed to the reversal of two decades of population decline'. At the same time, their practices of separation 'have brought them into conflict with former sect members, local residents and parts of the wider Western Australian population'.[42]

No issue has caused more commotion among Christian churches in recent years than child abuse. In a series of papers delivered at anti-cult, and some academic, conferences, British ex-Brethren IV and psychologist Jill Mytton claimed that by interviewing former members around the world she found that around 27 per cent of

---

41. Matthew Tonts, 'The Exclusive Brethren and an Australian Rural Community', *Journal of Rural Studies* 17 (2001): 309–322.
42. Tonts, 'The Exclusive Brethren and an Australian Rural Community', 321.

them claimed to have been sexually abused as children.[43] During the Charity Commission controversy, where Mytton was scheduled to be a witness before the case was settled, Brethren IV had her research examined by three academics, Konstantinos V. Petrides, Reader in Psychology and Psychometrics at the University College London (UCL); Adrian Furnham, Professor of Psychology, also at UCL; and Jane Hutton, Professor in Medical Statistics at the University of Warwick. They concluded that the self-selected sample and the leading questions made Mytton's research 'unscientific', and Furnham described it as a 'witch-hunt under the guise of scientific research'.[44]

Statistics about child abuse in religious groups are a notoriously controversial matter, and Brethren IV do not keep central records of members accused or convicted of any criminal activity, including child abuse. My search of media reports in Australia, New Zealand, and Europe found accounts of less than ten cases involving individual Brethren IV members investigated by the authorities. As it happens for other religious groups, there may be some other unreported cases. It is highly unlikely, however, that they are in the order of the hundreds, as Mytton's research would suggest.

Brethren IV certainly do not condone child abuse and have reacted to these cases by adopting measures, including a code of conduct that asks 'any report of alleged sexual abuse to be passed onto

---

43. Jill Mytton, 'The Mental Health of Second-Generation Adult Survivors (SGA) of the Exclusive Brethren: A Quantitative Study', paper presented at the Division of Counselling Psychology of the British Psychological Society Annual Conference, Cardiff, 12–13 July 2013.

44. Plymouth Brethren Christian Church, 'Sunday Star Times Article Based on "Unscientific" Discredited Study', media statement, 24 April 2016, available at http://www.plymouth-brethrenchristianchurch.org/wp-content/uploads/2016/04/160424-PBCC-Response-to-NZ-Sunday-Times1.pdf, last accessed 11 August 2016.

relevant authorities'.[45] It is also true that moral rectitude is a constant theme in Brethren IV ministry, doctrine, and church services. Comparative studies of cases in different religion communities by Anson D. Shupe and other scholars evidenced how child abuse is a problem existing in most religious institutions, and that reaction, in a way, always comes 'late', since churches do not believe that such a horrible tragedy may really affect them ('it can happen to others, but not to us'). As for the quality of the reaction, the measures introduced by Brethren IV, which crucially include provisions for reporting incidents to the secular authorities in accordance with the local laws, are not dissimilar in essence from the most recent provisions introduced by the Catholic Church that, when complied with, have significantly reduced the number of cases of abuse.[46] Teachers in Brethren IV schools, including those who are not Brethren, are also asked to comply with the child protection codes.[47]

THE PARADOX OF BRETHREN SCHOOLS

From the 1990s on, Brethren IV operate an impressive network of schools in several countries and today there are a total of 133 with 9,795 students attending. They are managed by committees of laypersons and not operated directly by the Plymouth Brethren Christian Church (PBCC). There are twenty-four 'campuses' in the United States and ten in Canada, part of the Sterling system; twenty-eight Focus Schools in the United Kingdom and three in Argentina;

45. Plymouth Brethren Christian Church, 'Sunday Star Times Article.'
46. Massimo Introvigne and Roberto Marchesini, *Pedofilia: una battaglia che la Chiesa sta vincendo* (Milan: Sugarco, 2014).
47. OneSchool Services, *Staff Handbook, Version 2* (Bowral, New South Wales: OneSchool Services, 2014).

thirty-four schools in Australia, fourteen in New Zealand, four in the Caribbean, sixteen in Continental Europe, including the Labora School in Sweden; several in France, and one recently opened near Rome. They offer different courses, from primary education up to high school.

My visits to Brethren IV schools in several countries confirmed the comments of Doherty and Dyason and Frisk and Nilsson.[48] They also evidenced a somewhat paradoxical situation. Parents and students are normally very happy with their experience in the schools. Non-Brethren teachers appreciate Brethren pupils as respectful and hard-working. The outcome of this positive environment is empirically measurable, and results in students in Brethren schools scoring higher than average in national tests.[49] Inspections, even when critical of other aspects, confirmed the high quality of Brethren IV education.[50]

Why, then, do Brethren IV schools come under frequent criticism? National situations seem to be somewhat different. In Australia, Brethren IV schools were involved in a national political controversy between those respectively favourable and hostile to state funding of private schools. Those who were against such funding used the campaigns against Brethren IV as a 'cult' to argue that the government was funding 'cult-related' schools, again despite the fact that students there score well, and in some case *very* well, in national tests.[51] It is worth noting that government funding only

48. Dyason and Doherty, 'The Modern Hydra'; Frisk and Nilsson, 'Raising and Schooling Children'.
49. Doherty, 'The Nurture and Admonition of the Lord'.
50. Frisk and Nilsson, 'Raising and Schooling Children', 350; Charles Moracchini, Sylviane Benoist and Noël Gorge, 'Rapport d'inspection d'établissement hors contrat Cours privé Les Cardamines, Z.A. Les Lebreyres, 43400 Le Chambon sur Lignon', 2014, copy in the archives of CESNUR (Center for Studies on New Religions), Torino, Italy.
51. Doherty, 'The Nurture and Admonition of the Lord'.

meets a small percentage of the considerable finance Brethren IV need to provide for their schools. The larger part comes from their community. In Sweden and France, criticism focused on the fact that children, although well prepared in curricular matters, were excluded from reading certain modern authors, using the Internet in a 'normal' way, and interacting with non-Brethren peers.

There was, however, a difference, as in Sweden, state inspectors criticised the Labora School, while in France criticism came from the official anti-cult agency MIVILUDES, influenced by local anti-cultists. While MIVILUDES regarded as suspicious the school in Le Chambon sur Lignon even before it was officially opened,[52] state inspectors praised the 'opening to children outside the community' and the 'cultural and sport relations with the territory'.[53] Sport, contrary to what some critics report, is normally practiced by Brethren students. In some countries, where several Brethren schools exist, they normally play against each other.

Both in Sweden and in Australia, libraries in Brethren IV schools were criticised for excluding certain contemporary authors. Certainly, books including sexually explicit passages are either excluded or censored. On the other hand, I personally found in school libraries well-read copies of 19th- and 20th-century classics, part of the general local curricula, including by authors such as Jane Austen and Emily Brontë, who are quite far away from Protestant fundamentalism. Doherty encountered repeatedly in Australian Brethren IV schools the book *Romulus My Father* by Australian philosopher Raymond Gaita, widely used in local high schools but not generally popular among conservative Christians for its candid discussion of extramarital affairs, mental illness, and

---

52. MIVILUDES, *Rapport au Premier ministre Année 2005*, 24.
53. Moracchini, Benoist and Gorge, 'Rapport d'inspection'.

suicide.[54] Doherty noted that the movie version of the novel was also available to students but in a censored version editing out the nudity.[55]

I found state-of-the-art computer technology in several Brethren schools, although Web contents were filtered. One objection by Swedish inspectors concerned gender stereotypes, reinforced by dress codes and running counter the strong emphasis on gender equality of the Swedish culture and school system.[56] The problem does not concern Brethren IV only, it is common to other conservative religious schools and raises questions on whether religious liberty includes the right to maintain an approach to gender issues based on conservative theological premises and different from mainline culture. Brethren IV schools, at any rate, have introduced programs against discrimination, harassment, and bullying.[57] As it happens for other Christian fundamentalists, Brethren schools are also accused of not teaching evolution. According to my observation and interviews, they do, although they present it as theory rather than as fact.

Swedish inspectors also complained that high school students were not adequately counselled in their choice of tertiary education, and that Brethren IV discouraged studies beyond the secondary level.[58] Similar concerns have been raised in other countries, including by Australian politicians. In this field, attitudes changed over time. Taylor Jr. advised against going to university, but apparently he believed that there was 'nothing wrong about education itself': 'if

54. Raymond Gaita, *Romulus My Father* (Melbourne: Text Publishing, 1988).
55. Bernard Doherty, personal communication, 2015.
56. Frisk and Nilsson, 'Raising and Schooling Children,' 353.
57. OneSchool Services, *Parents & Student Handbook, Version 3* (Bowral, New South Wales: OneSchool Services, 2014), 9–10; OneSchool Services, *Staff Handbook, Version 2*, 14.
58. Frisk and Nilsson, 'Raising and Schooling Children,' 352–353.

our children could go to college and not leave home, they would be that far safe.'[59]

In this field, as in others, Bruce Hales and his father, John S. Hales, adopted a more moderate position. They remained concerned about the possible immoral influences within campuses, yet recommended to pursue tertiary education through alternative courses. In fact, as early as in the 1960s, John S. Hales was advocating quality education for Brethren children. His programs have been continued by Bruce Hales, using modern tools such as self-directed learning and virtual classroom technology to reconcile the aim of achieving a world-class education wit concerns about the moral climate prevailing in certain public schools and colleges. Doherty concluded that 'little information is publicly available regarding the number of Brethren undertaking correspondence courses through tertiary providers, though anecdotal evidence suggests the numbers enrolled in university degrees remains small, and Vocational Education and Training (VET) sector training remains far more common. Nonetheless, this is still a significant, if incremental, shift in Brethren practice.'[60]

THE ELUSIVE PUBLIC BENEFIT AND
THE RAPID RELIEF TEAMS

'Public benefit' was at the very centre of the British Charity Commission case. There is little doubt that Brethren IV take care of the poor and mobilise significant humanitarian and charitable resources in cases of public calamities and wars. Unlike

---

59. Doherty and Dyason, 'Revision or Re-Branding?'; James Taylor Jr., *The Outpouring of the Holy Spirit* (Kingston-on-Thames: Stow Hill Bible and Tract Depot, 1960), 146.
60. Doherty and Dyason, 'Revision or Re-Branding?'

other Brethren communities and other groups, such as Jehovah's Witnesses, Brethren IV are not 'absolute' conscientious objectors. In war, they regard as their duty to support their government. During World War I, for example, Raven's daughter Emily volunteered as a nurse on the French front and was awarded a Royal Red Cross, second class. In principle, they should not take the life of others and, when legally possible, they ask to serve in non-combatant positions. In the past, however, some Brethren served in infantry, artillery, and cavalry, and a handful of them were killed in action.[61] More recently, pupils of British Brethren IV schools collected gifts and wrote letters to support British troops in Afghanistan.[62] Several Brethren businesses worked to support the war efforts, and this confirmed that Brethren IV, separated as they may be, interact with a wider audience through their business activities, not rarely of more than local importance. Brethren IV have a demanding work ethic. They work hard, and their businesses are often successful.

The initial Charity Commission's objection was that Brethren IV's charitable activities, as impressive as they may be, support only fellow Brethren IV and not those not in fellowship with their organisation. The historical record is a matter of dispute. Critics point out to statements by Taylor Jr. and others that each church should in principle take care of its own poor and there is no reason for Brethren IV to cooperate with charities outside the Church. Indeed, during the last four years of his life, Taylor Jr. felt that all the money he could personally give was needed for the Brethren Church, particularly for the benefit of its poorer members. During those years, he stopped giving to non-Brethren charities he had previously

61. Plymouth Brethren Christian Church, *Experiences of War* (Chessington, UK: Plymouth Brethren Christian Church, 2012).

62. Plymouth Brethren Christian Church, *Public Benefit* (Chessington, UK: Plymouth Brethren Christian Church, 2012), 28–29.

contributed to. He pointed out that, if every church would look after their own poor, there would be no problem with poverty in the world. Subsequent leaders encouraged charitable giving to non-Brethren charities to resume, as in earlier times, which Taylor Jr. had also encouraged for many years.

More generally, Brethren IV insist that from their very origins they devoted substantial time to charitable work, working tirelessly on behalf of the poor and the destitute of all denominations and faiths. On the other hand, apart from the early Brethren in Darby's time, it seems fair to state that for many years, for theological reasons grounded in their doctrine of separation, Brethren IV, while mobilizing their own charitable institutions in favour of all those in need, be they Brethren or not, cooperated rarely with charities outside their fold. However, this changed with John Hales and more definitely with Bruce Hales.[63] Both Australian and British Brethren IV collected and donated significant sums of money to several non-Brethren organisations, including the British Heart Foundation and the Red Cross.[64]

Although in previous years Brethren IV had already supported the homeless and the victims of natural disasters irrespective of their religious affiliation, Hales Jr. promoted a truly spectacular initiative in the shape of the Rapid Relief Teams, established in 2013. They are specialised units of Brethren who intervene in situations such as floods, fires, and earthquakes, and provide free meals to the homeless and the poor. Teams are active in Australia, New Zealand, the United States, Canada, the United Kingdom, and Continental Europe.[65] Increasingly, they include certified personnel specialised

---

63. Doherty and Dyason, 'Revision or Re-Branding?'

64. Plymouth Brethren Christian Church, *Faith That Serves* (Chessington, UK: Plymouth Brethren Christian Church, 2013), 62.

65. Information on their various activities can be found on the Rapid Relief Team website www.rapidreliefteam.org and in the corresponding Facebook page.

in first aid and other forms of emergency relief. They assist every-body, without inquiring about their religious opinions, as evidenced by their already mentioned intervention in 2016 after the Italian earthquake in a region where there are no Brethren. They received high praises for their activities in various countries. My interviews confirmed that Brethren IV are very enthusiastic about their Rapid Relief Teams and, considering their impressive achievements, often do not understand what the 'public benefit' question is all about.

Brethren IV do not proselytise for new members but regularly preach in the streets of the town and cities where they live and hand out their literature.[66] Although the public benefit of street preaching in general has been questioned, in my interviews Brethren IV reported cases where street preachers persuaded suicidal persons to change their mind, and of police authorities commenting favourably on the restraining effects of the practice.

CONCLUSION: TRADITIONAL VALUES IN A POSTMODERN WORLD

In 2012, Brethren IV reverted to their origins and decided to call themselves PBCC. The name has antecedents in Darby's early days, when he moved from Dublin to Plymouth, but also symbolically corresponds to Hales Jr.'s forward-looking program. Opponents immediately objected that it was merely a case of cosmetic rebranding, and they also insisted that Hales Jr.'s reforms were not sincere but were rather part of an international public relations campaign

---

66. The Brethren IV publishing house, Christian Doctrine and Gospel Publishing, supplies Bibles, Christian literature, and a large selection of Brethren ministry publications to the public, through a retail outlet at Chessington, London, and from their website christian-doctrineandgospelpublishing.org.

aimed to protect the legal, tax-exempt status of Brethren IV in various countries and to maintain state funding for the Church's schools in Australia.[67] Interestingly, Hales Sr. already described himself as a member of the Plymouth Brethren, when he was called up for military service in 1941 and had to complete his Mobilization Attestation Form.

Attributing merely cynical motivations to those who promote reform in a religious organisation is not uncommon, but it is unfair. If no reforms at all are introduced, the group is criticised. When reforms come, they are dismissed as mere public relations efforts. Of course, outsiders have no way of ascertaining Hales Jr.'s ultimate motivations for his reforms. These are, perhaps, not crucially important. The fact remains that reforms were implemented and introduced real changes in the Brethren communities and their relationships with society. This is not the conclusion of supposedly 'naïve' academics only. Suspicious governmental agencies, with a history of hostility to the Brethren, such as the British Charity Commission, came to the same conclusion more than once.[68]

Disaffected ex-members and those opposed to Brethren IV insist that a group that would not even share a meal with non-members, nor admit them to its main religious celebration, could not be really considered as operating for the public benefit. Here, however, the same behaviour is perceived in a very different way by Brethren IV and their critics. The question goes to the core of who Brethren IV are. They are the heirs of Darby, whose religious creativity managed to keep together two contradictory impulses. The first was the

---

67. Doherty and Dyason, 'Revision or Re-Branding?'
68. Charity Commission for England and Wales, *Preston Down Trust: Decision of the Commission*; Charity Commission for England and Wales, *Case Report Preston Down Trust (1155382).*

desire for Christian unity and for gathering all sincere Christians around the same table in anticipation of the rapture and of Christ's second coming. At the same time, 'apostate' churches were firmly described as in ruin and as part of 'Babylon', with the consequence that Brethren could not break bread with those who maintained direct or indirect relationships with them.

At first sight, these two impulses could not coexist, and the impression of many scholars of the Brethren is that Darby's successors, and Darby in his later years, finally privileged separation over desire for unity. This is, however, only part of the story. Darby, Raven, and the other leaders of Brethren IV did not operate according to a purely human, rational logic. Taylor Sr. was aware that the decision to practice primary and secondary separation made Brethren IV dangerously open to accusations of sectarianism. He answered in theological rather than human or sociological terms, by stating, 'the only thing that will save us from dropping down into a sect is to be on the Mount of Olives, so that we get everything spiritually.'[69]

But what, exactly, did 'being on the Mount of Olives' mean? Taylor Sr. explained in the same text that, when breaking bread in their assemblies, within themselves, the Brethren spiritually ascended to a higher ground, the 'Mount of Olives' from where they were to 'clothe with assembly thoughts' a much larger community, in a non-sectarian and ecumenical way. Thus, Brethren IV were breaking the bread *physically* only with the comparatively small number of those who were in fellowship with them. In a given city or town, they might be two or three only. *Spiritually*, however, Brethren IV broke bread 'not simply in relation to the two or three

---

69. James Taylor, Sr., *Ministry by J. Taylor*, 112 vol. (Kingston-on-Thames: Stow Hill Bible and Tract Depot, 1957–1969), 12: 14.

with whom we walk' but also in relation to a much larger ideal or spiritual assembly, 'otherwise we would be a sect'.[70]

An important leader of Brethren IV and a close associate of Taylor Sr., Charles Andrew Coates, commented: 'the most separate man is bound to be the widest man in sympathies, light and intelligence ... so that separation is the way to enlargement.'[71] Such a comment makes sense only from a theological point of view and only for the believer. In the divine economy, as interpreted by Brethren IV, separation works for the benefit of all sincere Christian believers, including those they feel unfortunately compelled to exclude, for biblical reasons, both from the Lord's Supper and from their ordinary meals. Brethren IV believe that their breaking of bread and way of life operate also for the benefit of many who are excluded from their fold and table. This is the ultimate, deeply theological root of Brethren's benevolence towards non-Brethren victims of poverty and disasters, from early initiatives in Darby's time to the Rapid Relief Teams. It also explains why the Brethren see no contradiction between this benevolence and their strict practice of separation.

On the one hand, Brethren regard as crucial for their testimony and mission to affirm their core values through a boundary maintenance system, of which they believe the principle of separation to be a necessary part. On the other hand, while maintaining a spiritual separation from the 'world', they offer a testimony of Christian spirit through their many charitable outreach activities.

Is separation admissible in the 21st century? Increasingly, this is becoming a legal and political rather than a merely religious or theological question. In 2012, Christian Harlang, a well-known Danish

---

70. Taylor, Sr., *Ministry by J. Taylor*, 12: 83.
71. Charles Andrew Coates, *An Outline of Mark's Gospel and Other Ministry* (Hampton Hill: Stow Hill Bible and Tract Depot, 1964), 472–473; Shuff, 'Open to Closed', 21.

lawyer specialising in human rights, provided the Brethren with a legal opinion on whether their right to practice separation was protected by international conventions as part of their religious liberty. Quoting studies by sociologists, Harlang noted that the principle of separation is not unique to the Brethren and is practiced by other Christian and Jewish communities. Separation also 'takes a central role in the beliefs of the Brethren religious community, and in the manifestation of their Christian religion.' Deriving from separation legal consequences adverse to the Brethren, including refusing to recognise their organizations as charities, would thus severely limit their religious liberty.

Harland admits that religious liberty is not absolute. International courts have recognised that it can be limited 'if the limitation of the right takes place in the interests of public safety, for the protection of public order, health or morals, or for the protection of the rights and freedoms of others.' Harlang, however, believes that none of these public interests are threatened by the Brethren's practice of separation.

He concludes:

Decisions that deny a religious group otherwise available and important rights and privileges based solely on the manner in which they practice their religion constitute a de facto interference with that group's ability to freely manifest their belief. The sole reservation on this must be that none of the proceedings made within the religious community could be contrary to basic norms of human behaviour. It is beyond doubt that the Brethren have a right to their doctrines and practices, including the principle of separation and the preclusion of non-members to participation of the Lord's Supper, and to refuse them charitable status and privileges such as are enjoyed by other religious groups, constitutes an interference with the freedom of religion as defined in the case law of the European Court of Human Rights.[72]

Separation may be unpopular and look somewhat bizarre in a culture emphasizing openness and relativism. However, Brethren IV's practice of separation has a clear religious basis. Whether a society is capable of accepting it becomes precisely a test for its real openness to religious liberty and tolerance.

The Brethren are fully persuaded that their firm adherence to the principle of separation should be protected by the international conventions on human rights. They ask to be allowed to follow their convictions within the framework of the fundamental freedoms of association, conscience, and religion. Brethren IV see themselves as Christians holding tenaciously to the truth of a light that they believe Darby received from Christ himself, separate from evil and yet witnesses to the Lord's death and resurrection, awaiting his second coming, in a rapidly evolving modern world.

They regard Darby as one who understood the true nature of the Church, linking back to Pentecost and the very beginnings of Christianity. They also believe that Darby was followed by leaders of like distinction as men of God, bringing out fresh truth on the meaning of Scripture, the Lord's Supper, and Christian life. From a small gathering of five believers in 19th-century Dublin to the present international movement led by Bruce Hales, they continue to offer a consistent Protestant critique of modernity and to jealously maintain Darby's core message as their most cherished heritage.

---

72. Christian Harlang, 'Legal opinion regarding the freedom of the Plymouth Brethren to their doctrinal belief in the principle of separation, including their right to preclude non-members from the Lord's Supper Service, according to current international human rights law' (Copenhagen: The Author, 2012), 5–6 and 17–18.

BIBLIOGRAPHY

A Brief Account of the Life and Labours of the Late W. J. Lowe. 1928. London: C.A. Hammond.

Acheson, Alan R. 1992. *A True and Lively Faith: Evangelical Revival in the Church of Ireland.* Dublin: Church of Ireland Evangelical Fellowship.

Adams, Norman. 1972. *Goodbye, Beloved Brethren.* Aberdeen: Impulse Books.

Akenson, Donald Harman. 2016. *Discovering the End of Time: Irish Evangelicals in the Age of Daniel O'Connell.* Montreal: McGill-Queen's University Press.

Anthony, Dick, and Massimo Introvigne. 2006. *Le Lavage de cerveau: mythe ou réalité?* Paris: L'Harmattan.

Bachelard, Michael. 2008. *Behind the Exclusive Brethren: Politics Persuasion and Persecution.* Melbourne: Scribe Publications.

Bebbington, David W. 1989. *Evangelicalism in Modern Britain: A History from the 1730s to the 1980s.* London: Unwin Hyman.

Bebbington, Eileen. 2014. *A Patterned Life: Faith, History, and David Bebbington.* Eugene (Oregon): Wipf and Stock.

Ben-Ezra, Juan Josafat [Manuel de Lacunza y Díaz]. 1827. *The Coming of Messiah in Glory and Majesty.* Edited and translated by Edward Irving. 2 vols. London: L.B. Seeley and Son.

Berzano, Luigi, and Massimo Introvigne. 1997. *Il gigante invisibile. Nuove credenze e minoranze religiose nella provincia di Foggia.* Foggia: NED.

Best, Brian, and Katie Stossel. 2006. *Sister Janet: Nurse and Heroine of the Anglo-Zulu War 1879.* Edited by Adrian Greaves. Barnsley (South Yorkshire): Pen & Sword Military.

Blackmore, John. 1860. *The London by Moonlight Mission: Being an Account of Midnight Cruises on the Streets of London During the Last Thirteen Years. With a Brief Memoir of the Author*. London: Robson & Avery.

Brocher, Émile. 1871. *Notice sur l'Église évangélique libre de Genève publiée à l'occasion du cinquantenaire de sa fondation*. Geneva: Église évangélique libre de Genève.

Bromley, David G., ed. 1988. *Falling from the Faith: Causes and Consequences of Religious Apostasy*. Newbury Park (California) and Beverly Hills (California): Sage.

Bromley, David G., ed. 1998. *The Politics of Religious Apostasy: The Role of Apostates in the Transformation of Religious Movements*. Westport (Connecticut) and London: Praeger.

Bromley, David G., and Anson D. Shupe, Jr. 1981. *Strange Gods: The Great American Cult Scare*. Boston: Beacon Press.

Bulteel, Henry Bellenden. 1831. *A Sermon on I Corinthians ii.12, Preached Before the University of Oxford, at St. Mary's, on Sunday, Feb. 6, 1831*. London: Hatchard & Son.

Buntain, William. 2016. 'The Exclusive Brethren and the Local Churches in China'. Unpublished manuscript.

Burnham, Jonathan D. 1999. 'The Controversial Relationship between Benjamin Wills Newton and John Nelson Darby'. PhD diss., University of Oxford.

Burnham, Jonathan D. 2004. *A Story of Conflict: The Controversial Relationship Between Benjamin Wills Newton and John Nelson Darby*. Eugene (Oregon): Wipf and Stock.

Campbell, R.[aymond] K.[enneth]. 1990. *Reunited Brethren: A Brief Historical Account Including a Brief Statement of Some Vital Principles of Faith*. Danville (Illinois): Grace & Truth.

Charity Commission for England and Wales. 2014. *Preston Down Trust: Decision of the Commission*. London: Charity Commission for England and Wales.

Charity Commission for England and Wales. 2016. *Case Report Preston Down Trust (1155382)*. London: Charity Commission for England and Wales.

Charles, Stanley. 1982. *The Church of God*. St. Louis (Missouri): Bible Truth Publishers.

'Clarence Esme Stuart: Biography'. N.d. Available at http://www.newble.co.uk/writers/Stuart/biography.html. Last accessed 9 August 2016.

Clark, Elmer Talmage. 1937. *The Small Sects in America*. Nashville (Tennessee): Cokesbury Press.

Coad, Frederick Roy. 1968. *A History of the Brethren Movement: Its Origins, Its Worldwide Development and Its Significance for the Present Day*. Exeter: Paternoster Press.

Coates, Charles Andrew. 1964. *An Outline of Mark's Gospel and Other Ministry*. Hampton Hill: Stow Hill Bible and Tract Depot.

Craik, Henry. 1863. *Principia Hebraica; or, Easy Introduction to the Hebrew Language, Exhibiting, in Twenty-four Tables, the Interpretation of All the Hebrews and Chaldee*

Words, Both Primitives and Derivatives, Contained in the Old Testament Scriptures. 2nd rev. ed. London: Samuel Bagster & Sons, and Bristol: W. Mack.

Cuninghame, William. 1813. *Pre-millennial Advent of Christ Demonstrated from the Scripture.* London: J. Hatchard.

Dann, Robert Bernard. 2004. *Father of Faith Missions: The Life and Times of Anthony Norris Groves (1795–1853).* Milton Keynes: Authentic Media.

Dann, Robert Bernard. 2006. 'The Primitivist Missiology of Anthony Norris Groves: A Radical Influence on Nineteenth-century Protestant Mission'. PhD diss, University of Liverpool.

Darby, John Nelson. 1841. *Reflections on the Ruined Condition of the Church, and on the Efforts Making by Churchmen and Dissenters to Restore It to Its Primitive Order.* London: G. Morrish.

Darby, John Nelson. 1866–1881. *Collected Writings of John Nelson Darby.* Edited by William Kelly. 34 vols. London: G. Morrish.

Darby, John Nelson. 1867. *Synopsis of the Books of the Bible.* New rev. ed. 5 vols. London: G. Morrish.

Darby, John Nelson. 1868. *The Notion of a Clergyman, Dispensationally the Sin Against the Holy Ghost.* London: G. Morrish.

Darby, John Nelson. 1886–1899. *Letters of John Nelson Darby.* Edited by John Alfred Trench. 3 vols. London: G. Morrish.

Darby, John Nelson. 1956–1971. *Collected Writings of John Nelson Darby.* 3rd ed. 34 vols. Kingston-on-Thames: Stow Hill Bible and Tract Depot, and Winschoten, The Netherlands: Heijkoop.

Darby, John Nelson. n.d. (circa 1941). *Letters of John Nelson Darby.* 3rd ed. 3 vols. Kingston-on-Thames: Stow Hill Bible and Tract Depot. First reprint, Winschoten, The Netherlands: Heijkoop, 1962–1963. Second reprint, Chessington, Surrey: Bible and Gospel Trust, 2005.

Darby, John Nelson. N.d. *Collected Writings of John Nelson Darby.* 2nd ed. Edited by William Kelly. 34 vols. (of which some might have been announced, but never published). London: G. Morrish.

Dates of J. N. Darby's Collected Writings. 2013. Chessington (Surrey): Bible and Gospel Trust.

Despins, Gilles. 2015. 'A Critical Assessment of J.N. Darby's Translation Work'. PhD diss., South African Theological Seminary.

DIMPAC (American Psychological Association Task Force on Deceptive and Indirect Techniques of Persuasion and Control). 1986. *Report of the APA Task Force on Deceptive and Indirect Techniques of Persuasion and Control.* Available at http://www.cesnur.org/testi/DIMPAC.htm. Last accessed 11 August 2016.

Doe, Norman. 2013. 'The Plymouth Brethren Christian Church: A Comparative Appraisal of Its Regulatory Framework'. Unpublished manuscript.

Doherty, Bernard. 2012. 'Quirky Neighbors or the Cult Next-Door? An Analysis of Public Perceptions of the Exclusive Brethren in Australia'. *International Journal for the Study of New Religions* 3, 2: 163–211.

Doherty, Bernard. 2013. 'The "Brethren Cult Controversy": Dissecting a Contemporary Australian 'Social Problem'. *Alternative Spirituality and Religion Review* 4, 1: 25–48.

Doherty, Bernard. 2015. '"The Nurture and Admonition of the Lord": Brethren Schooling and the Debate on Religious Schools in Australia'. Paper presented at the 2015 annual conference of CESNUR (Center for Studies on New Religions), Tallinn, Estonia, 17–20 June 2015. Available at http://www.cesnur. org/2015/doherty_brethren_tallinn_2015.pdf. Last accessed 11 August 2016.

Doherty, Bernard. 2016. 'The Brethren Movement: From Itinerant Evangelicals to Introverted Sectarians'. In *Handbook of Global Contemporary Christianity: Movements, Institutions, and Allegiance*, edited by Stephen Hunt. Leiden: Brill, 357–381.

Doherty, Bernard, and Laura Dyason. 2018. 'Revision or Re-Branding? The Plymouth Brethren Christian Church in Australia under Bruce D. Hales 2002–2016'. In *Radical Changes in Minority Religions*, edited by Eileen Barker and Beth Singler. Abingdon (UK) and New York: Routledge (forthcoming).

Donnelly, James S., Jr. 2009. *Captain Rock: The Irish Agrarian Rebellion of 1821–1824*. Madison: University of Wisconsin Press.

Dronsfield, W.[illiam] R.[oenals]. 1965. *The 'Brethren' Since 1870*. Lowestoft (Suffolk): The Author.

Dyason, Laura, and Bernard Doherty. 2015. 'The Modern Hydra: The Exclusive Brethren's Online Critics'. *St. Mark's Review* 233: 116–134.

Embley, Peter L. 1966. 'The Origins and the Early Developments of the Plymouth Brethren'. PhD diss., St. Paul's College, Cheltenham.

Embley, Peter L. 1967. 'The Early Development of the Plymouth Brethren'. In *Patterns of Sectarianism: Organisation and Ideology in Social and Religious Movements*, edited by Bryan R. Wilson. London: Heinemann Educational Books, 213–243.

Finke, Roger, and Rodney Stark. 1992. *The Churching of America, 1776–1990: Winners and Losers in Our Religious Economy*. New Brunswick (New Jersey): Rutgers University Press.

Flegg, Columba Graham. 1992. *'Gathered Under Apostles': A Study of the Catholic Apostolic Church*. Oxford: Clarendon Press.

Frisk, Liselotte, and Sanja Nilsson. 2017. 'Uppväxt och skolgång för barnen inom Kristna Kyrkan Plymouthbröderna: det svenska Perspektivet'. In *Guds nya barn-barn: Att växa upp i kontroversiella religiösa grupper*, edited by Liselotte Frisk, Sanja Nilsson and Peter Åkerbäck. Stockholm: Dialogos, 238–271.

Frisk, Liselotte, and Sanja Nilsson. 2018. 'Raising and Schooling Children in the Plymouth Brethren Christian Church: The Swedish Perspective'. In *Children in Minority Religions: Growing Up in Controversial Religious Groups*, edited by Liselotte Frisk, Sanja Nilsson, and Peter Åkerbäck. Sheffield (UK)—Bristol (Connecticut): Equinox, 333–361.

Fromow, George H.[azleton]. 1959. *B.W. Newton and Dr. S.P. Tregelles, Teachers of the Faith and the Future*. London: Sovereign Grace Advent Testimony.

Gaita, Raymond. 1998. *Romulus My Father*. Melbourne: Text Publishing.

Gallagher, Eugene V., ed. 2016. *'Cult Wars' in Historical Perspective: New and Minority Religions*. Abingdon and New York: Routledge.

Garton, Nancy. 1963. *George Müller and His Orphans*. London: Hodder & Stoughton.

Giorgi, Lorenza, and Massimo Rubboli, eds. 1988. *Piero Guicciardini (1808–1886): un riformatore religioso nell'Europa dell'Ottocento. Atti del Convegno di studi, Firenze, 11–12 aprile 1886*. Florence: Olschki.

Grant, Frederick W. 1897. *A Divine Movement and Our Path with God To-day*. Los Angeles: Good Tidings Publishers.

Grass, Tim. 2006. *Gathering to His Name. The Story of Open Brethren in Britain and Ireland*. Milton Keynes: Paternoster.

Groves, Anthony Norris. 1857. *Memoir of the Late Anthony Norris Groves, Containing Extracts from His Letters and Journals Compiled by His Widow* [Harriet Groves née Baynes]. London: James Nisbet & Co.

Haldane, James Alexander. 1852. *Memoirs of the Lives of Robert Haldane of Airthrey, and of His Brother, James Alexander Haldane*. London: Hamilton, Adams and Co.

Harlang, Christian. 2012. 'Legal opinion regarding the freedom of the Plymouth Brethren to their doctrinal belief in the principle of separation, including their right to preclude non-members from the Lord's Supper Service, according to current international human rights law'. Copenhagen: The Author.

Hempton, David—Myrtle Hill. 1992. *Evangelical Protestantism in Ulster Society, 1740–1890*. London: Routledge.

Introvigne, Massimo. 1995. 'The Secular Anti-Cult and the Religious Counter-Cult Movement: Strange Bedfellows or Future Enemies?' In *New Religions and the New Europe*, edited by Eric Towler. Oxford and Oakville (Connecticut): Aarhus University Press, 32–54.

Introvigne, Massimo. 2004. *Fondamentalismi. I diversi volti dell'intransigenza religiosa*. Casale Monferrato (Alessandria): Piemme.

Introvigne, Massimo. 2014. 'Advocacy, Brainwashing Theories, and New Religious Movements'. *Religion* 44, 2: 303–319.

Introvigne, Massimo, 2015. 'Who Is Afraid of the Plymouth Brethren? Brethren Controversies in Historical Perspective'. Paper presented at the 2015 annual conference of CESNUR (Center for Studies on New Religions), Tallinn, Estonia, 17–20 June 2015. Available at http://www.cesnur.org/2015/Brethren2015.pdf. Last accessed 11 August 2016.

Introvigne, Massimo, and Roberto Marchesini. 2014. *Pedofilia: una battaglia che la Chiesa sta vincendo*. Milan: Sugarco.

Introvigne, Massimo, and Domenico Maselli. 2007. *I Fratelli. Una critica protestante della modernità*. Leumann (Turin): Elledici.

'Italy—RRT Provide Meals for the Emergency Services at Operation Amatrice Aug 2016'. 2016. Available at http://www.rapidreliefteam.org/italy-rrt-provide-meals-for-the-emergency-services-at-operation-amatrice-aug-2016/. Last accessed 4 October 2016.

'Italy—RRT Serves Food at Avalanche Site, Rigopiano'. 2017. Available at http://www.rapidreliefteam.org/italy-rrt-serve-food-at-avalanche-site-rigopiano/. Last accessed 31 January 2017.

Jacini, Stefano. 1940. *Un riformatore toscano nell'epoca del Risorgimento: il conte Piero Guicciardini, 1808–1886*. Florence: Sansoni.

Kinnear, Angus Ian. 1973. *Against the Tide (The Story of Watchman Nee)*. Eastbourne (UK): Victory Press.

Lacunza y Díaz, Manuel de. 1969. *La Venida del Mesías en gloria y majestad*. Edited by Mario Góngora del Campo. Santiago de Chile: Editorial Universitaria.

Lewis, Donald, ed. 1995. *The Blackwell Dictionary of Evangelical Biography*. 2 vols. Oxford: Blackwell.

Lifton, Robert Jay. 1961. *Thought Reform and the Psychology of Totalism: A Study of 'Brainwashing' in China*. New York: W. W. Norton.

Madden, Hamilton (Mrs.) [Mary Elizabeth Anne Madden, née Moore]. 1875. *Memoir of the Late Right Rev. Robert Daly, DD, Lord Bishop of Cashel*. London: James Nisbet.

Maddox, Marian. 2011. 'The Church, the State and the Classroom: Questions Posed by an Overlooked Sector in Australia's Education Market'. *University of New South Wales Law Journal* 34, 1: 300–315.

Maddox, Marian. 2014. *Taking God to School: The End of Australia's Egalitarian Education?* Crows Nest (New South Wales): Allen & Unwin.

Maillebouis, Christian. 2013. 'Sur l'implantation du 'darbysme' en France au XXe siècle'. *Bulletin de la Société de l'histoire du protestantisme français* 159 (April–May–June 2013): 329–364.

Marinello, Thomas J. 2013. *New Brethren in Flanders: The Origins and Development of the Evangelische Christengemeenten Vlaanderen, 1971–2008*. Eugene (Oregon): Pickwick.

Marty, Martin E., and R. Scott Appleby, eds. 1991–1995. *The Fundamentalism Project*. 5 vols. Chicago and London: University of Chicago Press.

Maselli, Domenico. 1974. *Tra risveglio e millennio. Storia delle Chiese cristiane dei fratelli 1836–1886*. Turin: Claudiana.

Maselli, Domenico. 1978. *Libertà della parola. Storia delle Chiese Cristiane dei Fratelli 1886–1946*. Turin: Claudiana.

Maury, Léon. 1892. *Le Réveil religieux dans l'Église Réformée à Genève et en France (1810–1850). Étude historique et dogmatique*. Paris: Fischbacher.

Mauss, Armand. 1994. *The Angel and the Beehive: The Mormon Struggle with Assimilation*. Indiana and Chicago: University of Illinois Press.

Melton, J.[ohn] Gordon. 1985. *An Open Letter Concerning the Local Church, Witness Lee and the God-Men Controversy.* Santa Barbara (California): Institute for the Study of American Religion.

Melton, J.[ohn] Gordon. 1999. *Encyclopedia of American Religions.* 6th ed. Detroit: Gale.

Melton, J.[ohn] Gordon. 2003. *Encyclopedia of American Religions.* 7th ed. Detroit: Gale.

Melton, J.[ohn] Gordon. 2009. *Melton's Encyclopedia of American Religions.* 8th ed. Farmington Hills (Michigan): Gale Research.

Merritt, Chris. 2016. 'The Age Sued for Brethren Article'. *The Australian,* 18 July 2016.

MIVILUDES (Mission interministérielle de vigilance et de lutte contre les dérives sectaires). 2006. *Rapport au Premier ministre Année 2005.* Paris: MIVILUDES.

Moracchini, Charles, Sylviane Benoist, and Noël Gorge. 2014. 'Rapport d'inspection d'établissement hors contrat Cours privé Les Cardamines, Z.A. Les Lebreyres, 43400 Le Chambon sur Lignon'. Copy in the archives of CESNUR (Center for Studies on New Religions), Torino, Italy.

Müller, George. 1881. *A Narrative of Some of the Lord's Dealings with George Müller, Written by Himself.* 6 vols. London: The Author.

Mytton, Jill. 2013. 'The Mental Health of Second-Generation Adult Survivors (SGA) of the Exclusive Brethren: A Quantitative Study'. Paper presented at the Division of Counselling Psychology of the British Psychological Society Annual Conference, Cardiff, 12–13 July 2013.

Nason, Joy 2015. *Joy & Sorrow: The Story of an Exclusive Brethren Survivor.* Sydney: Centennial.

National Association of Evangelicals. N.d. 'What Is an Evangelical?' Available at http://nae.net/what-is-an-evangelical/. Last accessed 12 August 2016.

Neatby, William Blair. 1901. *A History of the Plymouth Brethren.* London: Hodder & Stoughton.

Newman, Francis William. 1856. *Personal Narrative in Letters, Principally from Turkey, in the Years 1830–1833.* London: The Author.

Newman, Francis William. 1874. *Phases of Faith; or, Passages from the History of My Creed.* 3rd ed. London: Trübner & Co.

Newton, Ken, and Jeanette Newton. 2015. *The Brethren Movement Worldwide: Key Information 2015.* Lockerbie (UK): OPAL.

Noel, Napoleon. 1936. *The History of the Brethren.* 2 vols. Denver: W.F. Knapp.

Noll, Mark. 2003. *The Rise of Evangelicalism: The Age of Edwards, Whitefield and the Wesleys.* Downers Grove (Illinois): InterVarsity Press.

Nunn, Philip. 2003. *The Re-Dividing of the Reunited Brethren: An Attempt to Diagnose.* Quindio (Colombia): Armenia.

OneSchool Services. 2014a. *Parents & Student Handbook, Version 3.* Bowral (New South Wales): OneSchool Services.

OneSchool Services. 2014b. *Staff Handbook, Version 2.* Bowral (New South Wales): OneSchool Services.

Ouweneel, Willem Johannes. 1976–1978. *Het verhaal van de broeders. 150 jaar falen en genade*, 2 vols. Aalten: Stichting Uit het Woord der Waarheid.

Partnership UK. 2013. 'News Release'. Available at http://www.partnershipuk.org/qwicsitePro2/php/docsview.php?docid=1659. Last accessed 9 August 2016.

Piepkorn, Arthur Carl. 1970. 'Plymouth Brethren (Christian Brethren)'. *Concordia Theological Monthly* 41: 165–171.

Pierson, Arthur Tappan. 1899. *George Müller of Bristol*. London: James Nisbet & Co. [2nd ed., 1907].

Plymouth Brethren Christian Church. 2012a. *Experiences of War*. Chessington (UK): Plymouth Brethren Christian Church.

Plymouth Brethren Christian Church. 2012b. *Public Benefit*. Chessington (UK): Plymouth Brethren Christian Church.

Plymouth Brethren Christian Church. 2013. *Faith That Serves*. Chessington (UK): Plymouth Brethren Christian Church.

Plymouth Brethren Christian Church. 2014. *Progression and Principles: The Plymouth Brethren Christian Church Today*. Chessington (UK): Plymouth Brethren Christian Church.

Plymouth Brethren Christian Church. 2016. 'Sunday Star Times Article Based on "Unscientific" Discredited Study'. Media statement, 24 April 2016. Available at http://www.plymouthbrethrenchristianchurch.org/wp-content/uploads/2016/04/160424-PBCC-Response-to-NZ-Sunday-Times1.pdf. Last accessed 11 August 2016.

Ratzinger, Joseph. 1966. 'Weltoffene Kirche?' In *Umkehr und Erneuerung. Kirche nach dem Konzil*, edited by Theodor Filthaut. Mainz: Matthias-Grünewald-Verlag, 273–291.

Raven, Frederick Edward. 1902. *Readings and Addresses in the United States*. Kingston-on-Thames: Stow Hill Bible and Tract Depot.

Raven, Frederick Edward. 1965–1968. *Ministry by Frederick E. Raven: New Series*. 21 vols. Kingston-on-Thames: Stow Hill Bible and Tract Depot.

Redekop, Bill. 2014. 'The Closed-Door Church: Inside the Secretive and Strict Plymouth Brethren Sect in Manitoba'. *Winnipeg Free Press*, 5 October 2014. Available at http://www.winnipegfreepress.com/local/The-closed-door-church-258336281.html. Last accessed 11 August 2016.

Richardson, James T. 1996. 'Sociology and the New Religions: "Brainwashing," the Courts, and Religious Freedom'. In *Witnessing for Sociology: Sociologists in Court*, edited by Pamela Jenkins and Steve Kroll-Smith. Westport (Connecticut) and London: Praeger, 115–137.

Ronco, Daisy Dina. 1986. *Per me vivere è Cristo. La vita e l'opera del Conte Piero Guicciardini nel centenario della sua morte*. Fondi (Latina): UCEB (Unione Cristiana Edizioni Bibliche).

Ronco, Daisy Dina. 1991. *Crocifisso con Cristo. Biografia di Teodorico Pietrocola Rossetti dalle lettere*. Fondi (Latina): UCEB (Unione Cristiana Edizioni Bibliche).

Rowdon, Harold Hamlyn. 1967. *The Origins of the Brethren, 1825–1850*. London: Pickering & Inglis.

Rowdon, Harold Hamlyn. 1986. *Who Are the Brethren and Does It Matter?* Exeter: Paternoster Press.

Rowdon, Harold Hamlyn. 1988. 'The Problem of Brethren Identity in Historical Perspective'. In *Piero Guicciardini (1808–1886): un riformatore religioso nell'Europa dell'Ottocento. Atti del Convegno di studi, Firenze, 11–12 aprile 1886*, edited by Lorenza Giorgi and Massimo Rubboli, op.cit., 159–174.

Salles, Rudy. 2014. *The Protection of Minors Against Excesses of Sects: Report*. Strasbourg: Council Europe, Parliamentary Assembly, Committee on Legal Affairs and Human Rights.

Shuff, Roger N. 1996. 'From Open to Closed: A Study of the Development of Exclusivism within the Brethren Movement in Britain 1828-1953'. B.D. diss., University of Wales.

Shuff, Roger N. 1997. 'Open to Closed: The Growth in Exclusivism amongst Brethren in Britain 1848-1953'. *Brethren Archivists and Historians Network Review* 1: 10–23.

Shuff, Roger N. 2005. *Searching for the True Church: Brethren and Evangelicals in Mid-Twentieth-Century England*. Bletchley and Milton Keynes: Paternoster Press.

Shupe, Anson D., Jr. 1995. *In the Name of All That's Holy: A Theory of Clergy Malfeasance*. Westport (Connecticut) and London: Praeger.

Shupe, Anson D., Jr.—David Bromley. 1980. *The New Vigilantes: Deprogrammers, Anti-Cultists, and the New Religions*. Beverly Hills (California) and London: Sage.

Shupe, Anson D., Jr. and David Bromley, eds. 1994. *Anti-Cult Movements in Cross-Cultural Perspective*. New York and London: Garland.

Singer, Margaret Thaler—Janja Lalich. 1995. *Cults in Our Midst*. San Francisco: Jossey-Bass.

Smith, Hamilton. 1967. *Perspectives on the True Church*. Minneapolis (Minnesota): Christian Literature.

Spini, Giorgio. 1971. *L'Evangelo e il berretto frigio. Storia della Chiesa cristiana libera in Italia, 1870-1904*. Turin: Claudiana.

Stott, Rebecca. 2017. *In the Days of Rain*. London: 4th Estate.

Stunt, Timothy C. F. 1976. 'John Synge and the Early Brethren'. *Christian Brethren Research Fellowship Journal* 28: 42–43.

Stunt, Timothy C. F. 1988. 'The Via Media of Guicciardini's closest collaborator, Teodorico Pietrocola Rossetti'. In *Piero Guicciardini (1808-1886): un riformatore religioso nell'Europa dell'Ottocento. Atti del Convegno di studi, Firenze, 11-12 aprile 1886*, edited by Lorenza Giorgi and Massimo Rubboli, op. cit., 137–158.

Stunt, Timothy C. F. 2000. *From Awakening to Secession: Radical Evangelicals in Switzerland and Britain 1815–1835*. Edinburgh: T. and T. Clark.

Stunt, Timothy C. F. 2004. 'Influences in the Early Development of John Nelson Darby'. In *Prisoners of Hope? Aspects of Evangelical Millennialism in Britain and*

Ireland, 1800–1880, edited by Crawford Gribben and Timothy C. F. Stunt, Eugene (Oregon): Wipf and Stock, 63–66.

Stunt, Timothy C. F. 2006. 'John Nelson Darby: Contexts and Perceptions'. In *Protestant Millennialism, Evangelicalism and Irish Society, 1790–2000*, edited by Crawford Gribben and Andrew Holmes, New York: Palgrave Macmillan, 83–98.

Stunt, Timothy C. F. 2015. *Early Brethren and the Society of Friends*. Eugene (Oregon): Wipf and Stock.

Symington, James Harvey. 1982. *How to Counter the Man of Sin*. (Vol. 107 of the J. H. Symington Ministry Collection). Kingston-on-Thames: Bible & Gospel Trust.

Taylor, James, Jr. 1960. *The Outpouring of the Holy Spirit*. Kingston-on-Thames: Stow Hill Bible and Tract Depot.

Taylor, James, Sr. 1925. *Christ's Personal Service for the Saints*. Auckland (New Zealand): Bible and Gospel Trust.

Taylor, James, Sr. 1956. *Letters of James Taylor*. 2 vol. Kingston-on-Thames: Stow Hill Bible and Tract Depot.

Taylor, James, Sr. 1957–1969. *Ministry by J. Taylor*. 112 vol. Kingston-on-Thames: Stow Hill Bible and Tract Depot.

Tchappat, David. 2009. *Breakout: How I Escaped from the Exclusive Brethren*. Sydney: New Holland Publishers.

The Beliefs and Practices of the Local Churches. 1978. Anaheim (California): Living Stream Ministry.

Thomas, Ngaire Ruth. 2005. *Behind Closed Doors: A Startling Story of Exclusive Brethren Life*. Auckland: Random House New Zealand.

Thompson, Paul, with Tony Wailey and Trevor Lummis. 1983. *Living the Fishing*. London: Routledge and Kegan Paul.

Tonts, Matthew. 2001. 'The Exclusive Brethren and an Australian Rural Community'. *Journal of Rural Studies* 17: 309–322.

'Two Laymen'. 1910–1915. *The Fundamentals: A Testimony to the Truth*. 12 vol. Chicago: Testimony Publishing Company.

U.S. District Court for the Northern District of California. 1990. 'Opinion (Jensen J.). Case No. CR-88-0616 DLJ. United States v. Steven Fishman,' 13 April 1990. 743 F. Supp. 713.

Vaucher, Alfred-Félix. 1935. 'Le Royaume de Dieu d'après le Père Lacunza'. *Les Signes des temps* 1: 7–15.

Vaucher, Alfred-Félix. 1941. *Une célébrité oubliée. Le père Manuel Lacunza y Díaz*. Collonges-sous-Salève: Fides.

Vaucher, Alfred-Félix. 1955. *Lacunziana. Essais sur les prophéties bibliques*. Collonges-sous-Salève: Fides.

Vinay, Valdo. 1961. *Evangelici italiani esuli a Londra durante il Risorgimento*. Turin: Claudiana.

Vinet, Alexandre. 1826. *Mémoire en faveur de la liberté des cultes*. Lausanne: The Author.

Ward, William R. 1992. *The Protestant Evangelical Awakening*. Cambridge: Cambridge University Press.

Ware, George W. 1931. *Later Contentions for the Faith*. Guildford: G.W. Ware.

Weber, Max. 1973. 'On Church, Sect, and Mysticism'. English transl. *Sociological Analysis* 34, 2: 140–149.

Wellershaus, Alfred. 2010. *Die Wahrheit Gottes und die Widerstände dagegen: Ein Überblick über die Geschichte der Brüder*. Gütersloh: Brüderbewegung. [1st ed., 1937]

Weremchuck, Max S. 1992. *John Nelson Darby*. Neptune (New Jersey): Loizeaux Brothers.

Wilson, Bryan R.[onald]. 1967. 'The Exclusive Brethren: A Case Study in the Evolution of a Sectarian Ideology'. In *Patterns of Sectarianism. Organization and Ideology in Social and Religious Movements*, edited by Bryan R. Wilson. London: Heinemann Educational Books, 287–342.

Wilson, Bryan R.[onald]. 1983. 'A Sect at Law'. *Encounter* 60, 1 (Jan.): 81–87.

INDEX OF PERSONAL NAMES